Longing to be Loved

Will their marriage survive their differences?

Allan and Jill Kennedy
as told to Kay Kuzma

Pacific Press Publishing Association
Nampa, Idaho
Oshawa, Ontario, Canada

Edited by Jerry D. Thomas
Cover photo by Stan Sinclair
Designed by Dennis Ferree

Copyright ©1997 by
Pacific Press Publishing Association
Printed in the United States
All Rights Reserved

Kennedy, Allan, 1950-
    Longing to be loved : can their marriage survive their
differences? / Allan and Jill Kennedy as told to Kay
Kuzma.
        p.   cm.
    ISBN 0-8163-1375-X (pbk. : alk. paper)
    1. Spouses—Religious life. 2. Marriage—Religious
aspects—Christianity.   3. Kennedy, Allan, 1950-
—Marriage.   4. Kennedy, Jill, 1954- —Marriage.
I. Kennedy, Jill, 1954- . II. Kuzma, Kay. III. Title.
BV4596.M3K46   1997
248.8'44'0922—dc21   96-37778
                                                       CIP

97 98 99 00 01 • 5 4 3 2 1

Contents

Dedication

To God, for His unfailing love and sustaining power.
Without Him, we would have no hope of making it!

And a heartfelt thanks to our two miracle boys,
Jeremy and Jonathan,
for your love and understanding
as we traveled our rocky road.
May you continue to reflect
God's extravagant love to others.

*P*rologue

It happened two thousand years ago. A woman crashed the party. The celebrities were all there: Simon, who had been healed of that dreaded disease leprosy; Lazarus, who had been raised from the dead; and Jesus, the guest of honor who had performed these incredible feats.

The guests crowded around, proud of the invitation to be part of this festive occasion, hoping to touch the miracle worker so they could go back to their friends and relatives and brag about it.

They all came for something. All, that is, except the woman. She came to give instead of to get. In her hands she held an alabaster box filled with the most costly perfume known in the world, spikenard, purchased with her life savings. Today, it might have been $30,000. One drop, maybe a thousand dollars' worth, would have filled the banquet hall with a fragrance that could not be contained, but she had not come to give one drop. She came to give her all.

She moved quickly to the honored Guest—the One to whom she owed her life—knelt down, broke her alabaster box, and with a heart overcome with gratitude and love, poured its contents on His head and feet. She had not thought about the outcome of her act. She only wanted to steal in, anoint Him, and quietly leave. But the aroma was startling even to her, and she began to wipe His feet with her hair.

You know the story. The words of criticism: "What a waste! It could have been sold and given to the poor!" And you know how Christ defended her with His response, "She has done a good work for Me. You'll always have the poor among you, but you won't always have Me." To paraphrase this for those who are married: "There will always be other people around, but you may not always have each other. That's why it's so important to love today. Love freely given is never wasted."

Fragrant acts—and fragrant words! That's the essence of unconditional love, of extravagant love. In our relationship, we had to decide whether or not to break our alabaster boxes for each other. Would we choose to love extravagantly? Or—afraid to risk—would we only give it drop by drop or withhold it altogether?

Like the woman who crashed the party two thousand years ago and broke her alabaster box, we had to weigh the cost against the potential gain. Could our marriage be saved? And if it could, was it worth the time and effort to make it work?

*P*rologue

Is extravagant love even possible between two people as different as we were? Only by traveling our rocky road could we find the answer.

Allan and Jill Kennedy

P.S. This is our story, told from our own points of view. It isn't our intention to hurt or offend anyone, and if we have inadvertently done so, please accept our apologies.

CHAPTER

1

In Pursuit of a Smile
Allan's Story

It was empty. For the thirteenth day in a row, my mailbox was empty. I had written *her* a letter every day for the last two weeks. With all the schoolwork I had to do, I really didn't have the time.

Logically, I figured that if I were sending a letter every day, I should be getting a response at least every other day! Now thirteen days had gone by—and nothing. I sighed and turned to retreat to my dorm room and lick my wounds. There wasn't much sense in my writing to some cute young thing if she wasn't going to write back—smile or no smile!

Maybe after meeting her in the cafeteria I had assumed too much during the week we had spent together on the campus of Middle Tennessee State University in Murfreesboro. I recalled the time I first had seen her. What a smile! She flitted around the cafeteria like a butterfly, chatting with first one, then another, laughing, eyes sparkling, giggling—I just couldn't forget that smile. Yet there was no way I could speak to a stranger!

After I first noticed this olive-skinned, dark-eyed beauty, I couldn't squelch the anticipation that built in my heart each time I neared the cafeteria. Would she be there again? The third time I saw her, I realized that her smile was beginning to mean far more to me than the general physics and quantitative analysis that I was trying to cram into my brain during an intensive summer-school session between my junior and senior year of college.

What happened next was as much a surprise to me as it would have been to anyone who knew me at that time, for I was bashful. I was worse than bashful—I was terrified of going up to somebody I didn't know and introducing myself, let alone trying to carry on a conversation.

But I had to know who she was. Summer-school students were a fickle crowd, coming and going. Any day might be her last, and I could never have lived with myself if I were to let her flit away without at least knowing her name and address. So as I slowly ate my meal, I began to plan how I would do it. Bite by bite, I watched as she sat with her friends at the table. She was dressed in cute red shorts and a white sleeveless blouse. My plate was finally emptied, even though I had no idea what I ate. Still I sat, rehearsing what I was going to say, not yet able to move, pushing my fork around on the plate's empty surface, trying to summon up enough courage to walk across the immense distance of some thirty feet of cafeteria floor to meet this girl with the smile.

Finally, I could procrastinate no longer, or the opportunity would be lost. I picked up my tray, clenched it tightly in front of me as if it were a shield that would somehow protect me from the pain of the contact I was about to make, and with slow deliberation approached the object of my desire, watching her waist-length black hair bounce as she laughed and tossed her head.

As I came up to her, I took a deep breath, and after all that practice simply said, "Hi, my name is Allan. What's yours?"

To which she replied, "Why do you want to know?"

I should have known then. I should have given up and gone back to my quantitative analysis book. But instead, I stood there completely taken aback. I had seldom been at a loss for words before. I have a quick mind. I'm a man who is in charge of his life, yet I had nothing to say.

She continued to play with me as a cat does with a mouse, "Tell me again, what is your name? What are you doing here?"

I caught my breath and answered like a witness facing interrogation, "I'm a senior at Southern College near Chattanooga, taking general physics and "quant" at MTSU this summer so I can graduate next spring."

I could tell something was happening behind that smile. She appeared somewhat taken aback. Was she impressed? Or was she merely trying to figure out a way to dispose of me? It was neither. She plainly didn't believe me. "Show me your ID," she said.

Moments before, I had rehearsed various ways the conversation might go, but somehow I hadn't anticipated this. Later, I chastised myself for not thinking of some clever retort, but, instead, I merely put down my tray, opened my wallet, and produced my student ID card.

After close scrutiny, she seemed to accept it as legitimate and thus began our mealtime meetings at the cafeteria. The next few days were heaven—the anticipation, the sight of her waiting, drinking in her every word and bathing in the warmth of her contagious smile. And then it was over. She promised to write, and she did for a while. But since the fall semester had started with me at Madison Hospital near Nashville doing my clinical rotation for Southern's Medical Technology program, the letters slowed and had now stopped.

As I reflected on how gullible I had been to fall so hard, so fast, and to believe that I might have meant something to her, I decided that turnabout was fair play. If she wouldn't write, neither would I.

However, sixty empty mailbox days later, I didn't like the feel of the empty place in my heart. If she wouldn't write, at least I had to talk to her. Having little money, I seldom called anyone long distance, but swallowing my pride, I dialed her home number, fully intent on giving her a piece of my mind. Her mother seemed happy to hear from me and explained that Jill was very ill and was in the hospital.

Abruptly, my mood shifted. The lecture I had been preparing to deliver because of her neglect to correspond melted into puddles of concern. As soon as the week's classes were finished, I showered and shaved, went to the florist, spent my life savings on a bouquet of roses, and headed "Old Blue," my '64 Chevy, toward Rockwood.

The parking lot of Chamberlain Memorial Hospital was filled with cars. I found a spot and wondered who all those people could be visiting. It didn't take me long to find out. As I headed down the hall, I could tell immediately which room was Jill's. The buzz of talk and the sound of laughter grew as I neared Room 243. I finally gathered courage and stepped through the door, pushed my way to her bed, and handed her the flowers.

Suddenly, everything was OK again. I made it clear that I had come a long way and wasn't planning to leave for some time. So, slowly her other friends drifted away, leaving us alone. She then turned to me, and with that magic smile—weakened only slightly by illness and fatigue—said, "I'm hungry. I would sure love some chicken noodle soup."

At that moment, if she had asked for the moon, I would have figured out a way to bring it to her. She gave me directions to the B and J Cafe on Front Street, where they made the best chicken noodle soup in town—and I was off on my quest. Moments later, I returned. She ate it all, and that was the beginning of her recovery—and of my love affair with this enchanting dark-haired beauty.

2

How Will I Know It's Love?

Jill's Story

I had always had a lot of boyfriends. I wasn't very studious in high school, but I guess you'd say I was popular. I was dating the captain of the football team, and I'd just been nominated for Homecoming Queen. Along the way, I had been in the Roane County Beauty Pageant and was first runner-up. I was editor of the school annual, and as office assistant to the high-school secretary was trusted with carrying the money to the bank on a daily basis. I'd been selected as the most dependable member of my senior class. I held numerous club offices and knew everyone.

Things were really moving along. I had a long-term goal to become rich and famous, but as a senior, I had already reached my major short-term goal—to be one of the most popular people in my high school. More specifically, I was on a roll to beat Sharon Givens as Homecoming Queen, and the way things were going, my chances were good.

I guess as I look back at my high-school career, it's quite apparent why I wasn't on the honor roll. Obviously, I was too busy trying to be Miss Popularity, and the popular kids weren't exactly Einsteins.

How lucky could I be? Mike, my football hero, was head-over-heels in love with me. He catered to my every whim. He bought me whatever I wanted—jewelry, music boxes, candy—nothing was too good for me. Not only was he captain of the football team but he was an all-around nice guy—a real gentlemen. We were really made for each other, and everyone else thought so too. He was a good Christian, shared the same belief system I did, and we went to church together. My whole family adored him. My friends thought we were the ideal couple. But in spite of all this, something inside me just didn't feel right. In his view, I was the one and only, and although he never told me, I'm quite sure his plans included immediate marriage after we graduated from high school.

During this time I was so confused. I remember going to my mother and asking, "How will I know it's love? How will I know whether Mike is the right person for me?"

I didn't want to make a mistake. My parents showed little affection to each other publically. At times I felt a cold wind of indifference blowing in our house, and I had the feeling there were some underlying problems in their relationship. It seemed to me as if they weren't in love. But it wasn't until a year later that my suspicions were confirmed.

Dad left and filed for divorce.

My mother came from an abusive family, but she was determined to break the cycle. We three kids were taught to be happy and optimistic. Neither of my parents came from a religious background, but my mother was trying very hard to do everything right—to give us everything she didn't have as a child. So we faithfully went to church every Sunday and came home to a chicken dinner, where the blessing was said. Then at bedtime, she would repeat with us, "Now I lay me down to sleep . . ." She took me to Sunbeams and G.A.s (Girl's Association), where we learned Bible verses. But for me, these religious acts were more ritualistic in nature than rooted in a personal experience with Christ.

My older sister, Judy, was the goody-goody in our family. She never did anything wrong. But with my naturally mischievous tomboy nature, I was always in trouble. I don't know, maybe it was just the way I figured out how to get attention, since I was the middle child and my mom was always working. My brother, John, was the quiet, gentle, studious one. He was six years younger—and far too good to be a boy! I hated it when he arrived on the scene, because as the first grandson in the family, he stole my favored position among the relatives.

I never had any training for marriage. In this relationship with Mike, who seemed like the ideal person, I kept wondering why it just didn't feel right. I was a romantic, and I wanted to feel the bells and whistles going off when a guy whispered my name or touched me. But all my mom said as she replied to my question about love was, "You will know. You will just know."

I really struggled with that; I wanted a list. I wanted objective evidence that Mike was meant for me, but I was left in limbo.

It was the summer between my junior and senior year when the direction of my life took a drastic turn. I realized my junior year that being in the band was the way to rub shoulders with the most popular kids in school, and at the same time it meant a free ticket to all the football games in which Mike played. I wanted desperately to be accepted, yet I didn't want to discipline myself to practice a musical instrument. That seemed like too much work and not enough fun. So I decided to try out for the flag corp. I was immediately chosen captain of the corp. But that was short-lived. At the biggest game of the season, when Rockwood High was playing our rival, Kingston, I, Nina Jill Evans, eternal sanguine, led the corp one way while the band went the other—and I was immediately demoted to assistant under the able leadership of a choleric!

Now it was June, and the flag corp was going to MTSU in Murfreesboro for a week of intensive training in marching and twirling. This was not my idea of having fun! It was hot and sticky, and the long days were filled with marching and being drilled under the blazing sun. It was the first time I had ever had a sunburned nose, and was it ever burned!

Lunchtime was our only reprieve from this grueling, torturous workout. I was just like all the other giggling girls, who kept one eye on what they were eating and the other on the eligible male college student population. Then it hap-

2—L.B.L.

17

pened. This good-looking, dignified, well-dressed stranger approached our table. I thought, "He's here to talk to Carol Ann"—the majorette sitting across the table from me. The majorettes, I felt, were a step higher than the flag corp. All the guys wanted them. I would have tried out for being a majorette if it hadn't taken so much work—or money—since my family hadn't had the means for me to take dance and baton lessons when I was younger. So here I was in the flag corp with this handsome guy approaching the table. He stepped up beside me and spoke. When I realized he was speaking to me, I turned in surprise.

Then it happened—the bells began ringing, and the whistles blew. It took only moments for me to realize that I had a new goal in life. This was the one! But I couldn't let him know I was interested. When he invited me to the college rec hall, I knew I had arrived. I was the only high-school girl in an entire building filled with university students. To top off that wonderful evening, he brushed my lips with a gentle kiss as he said goodbye at the dorm. Talk about bells and whistles! Wow!

I immediately ran into the dorm and called my mother and told her I had met the one and only. "This is it," I shouted, "This is the one."

I was so smitten, I couldn't eat for the rest of the week. I must have lost five pounds!

Then four days later, I was leaving. He waved as our bus headed back to Rockwood. But in my heart I treasured the promise we had made to write each other. I was true to my promise during the summer, since I had little else to do, but when my senior year began, the flurry of activities left me winded. There was also the problem of what to do with Mike. I decided to break up, and the minute I did, chaos reigned. The coach came and pled with me, because Mike wasn't performing as he should. Then, with Mike out of the picture, other boys suddenly inundated me with invitations and dates. The principal had warned me to watch out for those college guys, and to top off all that I was experiencing, when the guidance counselor found out that Allan was an Adventist, he began telling me Adventist jokes. So in spite of the feelings I had for Allan, confusion returned. I started dating around and quit writing. By Christmastime, as a consequence of my flirtatious behavior, the stress from family, and my overloaded schedule, my resistance went down, and I ended up in the hospital with "mono."

I was very, very sick. I remember the doctors had even said that if I wouldn't eat, I could die. But I had no appetite and was far more interested in all the attention my illness was bringing me than in food. My classmates felt sorry for me. They no longer were calling me "Heartbreaker" but were showing me genuine concern. And then, with my room full of friends whose approval and attention I so craved, in came Allan, flowers in hand. I took one look and heard the bells again. I thought, *Wow—roses! This is the one*. But I struggled. I had already given up being Homecoming Queen because of Allan. Everyone said that if I had still been dating Mike, I would have been a sure winner. What more would I have to give up? One by one, my friends left the hospital room, leaving me alone with Allan Kennedy. Suddenly I was hungry. I was starved for chicken noodle soup. Chicken noodle soup for my heart!

3

Unequally Yoked

(Jill) A few days later, Allan sent a bouquet to my hospital room—a basket of daisies and wildflowers. This simple gesture of thoughtfulness made my heartstrings tug in his direction.

Finally, I was released from the hospital. The doctor prescribed a two-month recuperation period with lots of rest and a homebound teacher. Allan began visiting, making the two-hour trip from Madison (where he was finishing his clinical year in medical technology) to Rockwood as often as his work and class schedule would permit.

A few days before Christmas, I was still weak but not too weak to say Yes when Allan invited me to his home in Columbus, North Carolina, to meet his family.

What an experience that was. I shall never forget the

lifestyle contrast between our families. We had TV, watched the latest movies, and ate the normal American diet. They had no TV, didn't go to movies, and were vegetarians.

His folks exhibited an attitude of warm congeniality and open communication. Mine didn't talk much. They didn't argue, but at times you could feel the draft of a cold war going on between them. His sisters looked like something out of Louisa Mae Alcott's *Little Women* or Laura Ingalls Wilder's *Little House on the Prairie*. I was captivated by the simplicity of this family. The wholesome lifestyle I saw them living was something I wanted. What a contrast to the shallowness of my values.

But I couldn't stand the food. I had grown up on chicken noodle soup, ham sandwiches, and hamburgers with a Dr. Pepper! I had such a craving for "real" food that on Saturday night I couldn't stand it any longer and began to complain to Allan. So, without telling his folks why we were leaving (I didn't want to hurt them), Allan took me twenty-six miles to the closest Shoney's. I don't remember much about the food at Shoney's, but I do remember Allan winking at me across the table. Our romance was building.

But with each new discovery about Allan, I realized the incredible differences in our family backgrounds, our interests, and our religious convictions.

Allan had been taught to work hard. I tried hard never to work or at least to turn it into a fun adventure. At home, I would even roller skate while doing the dishes, with my mother yelling, "Jill, you're going to break those dishes."

Allan was a gardener. But when my mother sent me out to the garden for radishes, I came back empty-handed. I had no idea they grew below the ground. I was looking for them above ground.

Allan could cook. The only things I knew how to cook were pork chops, meatloaf, and chicken. And he didn't eat those.

Allan was very studious and an avid reader. I enjoyed playing ball and having fun with my friends.

Allan was as true as the needle was to the pole. I tended to stretch the truth to conveniently cover my perceived inadequacies. Allan would warn me, "Jill when you stretch the truth, you've got to be careful of the snapback."

Allan was disciplined and punctual. I was not. I had a bus ticket to Allan's brother's wedding, where Allan was to be the best man, and I thought I had heard what time the bus was to leave but never even checked the ticket. I was only an hour late! Allan, as best man, left the wedding preparations, raced from Columbus over the Smokies to Knoxville to pick me up, and raced back, barely making it in time to walk into the church with his brother.

Allan was an early riser. I slept in as long as possible—unless there was something fun going on.

Allan was an introvert. I enjoyed being the center of attention.

Allan was a Seventh-day Adventist and went to church on Saturday. I was a Baptist and couldn't understand why anyone would want to go to church on the day the world played, while the rest of the world kept Sunday.

Allan was focused and goal-oriented. He knew exactly what he wanted to do in life. He was going to get through school and be an administrator. I was still smelling the roses.

His was a work ethic—mine one of pleasure!

(Allan) Jill is absolutely right. We were as different as night and day. My family was organization personified. I was the oldest of four—two boys and two girls—each born about two years apart.

Work was about all I knew growing up. My mom made lists for us kids before we could even read by illustrating the activities we were to do with pictures she drew. Every day we were expected to check off the required tasks.

I graduated from cleaning the sink and commode and making my bed to doing the dishes, caring for the animals, and mowing the lawn. When my brother and I left for academy, my dad had to buy a bush hog and tractor just to keep up with the mowing we had been doing.

One day, several large crates were delivered to our home filled with strawberry plants Dad had ordered. He had borrowed a tractor and dug a half-mile irrigation ditch so we could irrigate the field in front of the house, where we planted the strawberries to supplement the family income. Picking strawberries was a lot of work that next year, but our reward—strawberry shortcake three times a day for several weeks—was wonderful!

With the birthday and Christmas money I had saved, I bought some chicks, raised them, and sold eggs, keeping my accounts in a little brown spiral notebook. I can remember coming home late but still going out to make sure the chickens had water and were closed in their pen for the night. Our grandfather, Pops Klady, who lived several miles away, gave us orphan lambs, which we bottle fed and kept as pets. We had an old horse, Maude, that we used to pull a wagon and cut trails to drive on. Dad called her a "quarter" horse, with three feet in the grave and one out! In order to feed her, we planted a small field of corn, cultivated it with a horse-drawn cultivator, and shocked it in the fall for winter feed.

We ate lots of lentils, the northern equivalent of pinto beans. I wore shirts made out of flour sacks. The only clothes we bought were shoes, socks, and underwear.

We didn't get a lot of gifts as kids. The first present I really remember was a wooden truck my dad made for me. It was painted fire-engine red, with a nail for a steering wheel—a boy's dream. One Christmas we children were asked, "If you could have anything you wanted, what would it be?" I chose a big erector-type set. A dentist's family had adopted our family as their Christmas project and gave each of us kids the gift we had selected. It wasn't until years later that I found out who had been our Santa Claus.

Although we were probably classed as poor, we didn't realize it. When I was around ten, my folks built a small, private-pay rest home. Dad and Mom would get up before daybreak to cook breakfast for the guests. We children helped cook, served food, cleaned, did the laundry, and, after the residents were served, ate our meals there. Holidays were celebrated with the residents. Because of the rest home, we didn't vacation or travel much. The focus of our family was to make a living, so responsibility was far more important than pleasure.

I worked hard to earn a little extra money mowing the dentist's lawn and working for Pops Klady, harvesting vegetables and picking fruit. I took pride in my work, and Pops said I was the best helper he'd ever had. He was particular—nothing green, nothing rotten. With my choleric perfectionism, I exceeded his expectations.

As a high school student attending Fletcher Academy, a Seventh-day Adventist boarding school, I was given the job of managing the school's service station garage. I carried this responsibility so capably that the work supervisor persuaded the faculty council to let me graduate in three years so I could continue managing the garage for him. With school during the day (crowding four years into three) and paying my own way by working at the garage, being night watchman, and bagging groceries at Bi-Lo on Fridays, I found my security in what I could accomplish.

Next to work, church was a central focus in our lives. We regularly had morning and evening family worship. The only time I can ever remember missing church was when I was nine. I was asked to go with a Pathfinder group, our church's equivalent to Boy Scouts, on a campout, because my dad had found the camping spot for them. We were rained out and ended up having to go back to the basement of my folk's rest home to spend the night because they hadn't brought any rain gear. I slept in my own bed. The next morning, which was Sabbath, my folks said that instead of going to church, I should spend the day with the Pathfinder group, since they were guests of mine. Not only did I get religion at home and church but I also got it every day at the church school I attended.

I didn't date much in high school, because the asking was so painful and because, with my study and workload, I really didn't have the time. While in college, I knew most of the students by name and dated many of the girls, but nothing of lasting interest developed. Now as I finished my senior year at Southern College and was planning to go to graduate school at Loma Linda University (both church schools), my mom was trying subtly to turn my interests away from Jill. She had real concerns about my friendship with Jill, wanting me to marry a good Seventh-day Adventist girl who would have values similar to the Kennedy family.

I remember, just before graduation, that Mom and I were in the women's dorm, and Mom was making comments about the nice qualities of some of the girls in the dormitory.

"Allan, look how nice that girl is!" she would say. Finally, in exasperation, I spouted, "Well, maybe I don't like nice girls." Instantly, I realized how hurtful those words were. She had only my best interests at heart.

Being equally yoked was a basic principle I had grown up with. I knew how important it was, for a successful marriage, to have the same religious beliefs. I valued the similar religious interests and attitudes of my folks, and I enjoyed the benefits of being part of a family that went to church and worshiped together. But at this moment, I felt an irresistible tugging toward Jill. Later, I found a definition of romance that aptly describes what I was feeling at that time. "Romance is a temporary blinding of the factual thought processes just long enough that marriage can occur."

4

Getting Together

(Jill) What the Kennedys didn't realize was what an incredible impression their committed Christian family had made on my family—especially my twelve-year-old brother, John. When Allan came to visit me on weekends, John was the typical little brother who spied on us from behind the couch and flipped the porch light when he thought we had been outside long enough. But beyond this, John looked up to Allan. He was fascinated with Allan's religious beliefs. From the time John was a little boy, he had always asked questions and had a spiritually sensitive spirit. He had never been content with Sunday keeping and had questioned my parents about why we didn't go to church on the seventh day as it said we should do in the Ten Commandments. Now Allan was able to give him answers to his long-standing questions.

I was more concerned at that moment about surviving my senior year as "Miss Popularity." I had begun to see my ratings drop as my friends could not understand how I could be so disloyal as to jilt Rockwood's football captain for some out-of-town college guy. My bout with "mono" also hadn't helped. Being hospitalized for a number of weeks and then homebound for two months, I wasn't able to nurture my friendships as I had previously done, and rumors began to crop up about why I had been out of school so long—some wondering if I were pregnant! My mind was totally absorbed in surviving the year with as much popularity as possible.

After graduation, I was able to focus more on my future and what I wanted out of life. I was happy with the attention from Allan and had my heart set in that direction, but he was in graduate school two thousand miles away at Loma Linda University in Southern California, and I had a life to live. So I got a job at the Holiday Inn and decided to attend community college.

During this time, John's interest in religion began to spill over to me. Even my mom showed an interest. She had recently heard that her ancestors had been seventh-day Sabbath keeping Waldensians who had moved to Walden's Ridge near Spring City, Tennessee. One day she found an ad in the paper that said the local Adventist church had a new pastor, and she asked if we would like to go and meet him. Once we attended, Pastor Glenn Mitchell took a real interest in our family. He visited our home and started Bible studies with us. When John and I began to be convicted about Sabbath observance, Pastor Mitchell's home became a quiet Sabbath refuge for us away from the blaring TV sporting events to which my dad was addicted. Mrs. Mitchell began showing me how to prepare healthy vegetarian dishes. The pastor's interest in our whole family was demonstrated by biking with us on Sabbath afternoons to the next town to visit Mom, who was working at the Holiday Inn.

As the weeks passed, our commitment to keep the seventh-day Sabbath increased, and we decided to be baptized. Allan had no idea about our decision to join the Adventist church. Pastor Mitchell, knowing about my interest in Allan, arranged a surprise meeting with the Kennedy family, who were at the time attending a special program at Little Creek Academy, the Seventh-day Adventist boarding school Allan's sister was attending. I'll never forget the moment we told them the news. We were sitting on a beautiful lawn underneath lush green pines when Pastor Mitchell made the announcement that John and I were going to be baptized on November 11, Allan's twenty-second birthday. I was eighteen. Suddenly Allan's mother saw me in a whole new light. No longer did my relationship with Allan threaten the dreams she held for her son or the values that the Kennedy family held dear.

The day after our baptisms, Mom Kennedy called Allan and said, "Jill's OK. We went to her baptism yesterday— and I believe she will be a nice girl for you."

At the time I had met Allan, I did not perceive my hunger for spiritual things. Little did I realize how God was leading in my life to prepare me for what I would be facing in the days ahead. My idea that success was winning the popularity contest was shallow. "Mono" had a devastating effect on my plans, and after my friends scattered for the summer, I had time to refocus. It's a good thing I did, or I would not have been spiritually ready for what was to happen a week after my baptism.

The next weekend was perhaps the highest and lowest point in my life. I was asked to share my testimony at a Church Ministries convention at a local retreat center. What an exhilarating experience! Not only did I hear great inspirational messages, but I made new acquaintances with teens my age who made me feel loved and accepted in this new faith. But when I returned home after that spiritually high weekend, I was devastated to learn that my father had moved out, and my parents were planning to get a divorce. I had not perceived that there was that big of a problem—after all, they had been married for twenty-two years.

I knew their marriage had been arranged by my maternal grandmother, and I know I would have resented being yanked out of high school and forced into a relationship. With this start, it seems they had lived as married singles for most of their wedded lives. I determined this would never happen to me!

The finality of divorce ripped away my security. As the weeks passed, I found it almost impossible to study for my college courses as I worried about what would happen to Mom and Dad—as well as us kids. Without Dad's income, I felt the need to help Mom pay the bills. But could I find enough work?

When I was baptized and announced to my supervisor

at the Holiday Inn that I could no longer work from Friday night sundown to Saturday sundown, she said she couldn't assure me that I would have much work. But incredibly, God provided. Without asking, I was trained as a hostess, cashier, and waitress, and I was offered more work than I was able to take. But working more meant less time to study, and I eventually dropped out of college.

Always in the back of my mind, I knew there was Allan. I loved him. But would he ever propose?

(Allan) I had always believed that when you marry, you marry for life and that you marry the family. So it was important not to make a mistake. I realized that even though I loved Jill and that we could probably make it even if unequally yoked, going ahead with marriage without the approval and acceptance of my family would be a major handicap. Plus, I was so grounded in living according to God's instructions—including keeping the fourth commandment that said, "the seventh day is the Sabbath of the Lord your God" (Exodus 20:10) and His counsel about not being unequally yoked (2 Corinthians 6:14)—that whenever Jill would bring up the idea of marriage, I tended to avoid the subject.

I hesitated to come right out and say how important it was to me that we have similar religious beliefs. I didn't want her to become a Seventh-day Adventist just to marry me. If she was the one with whom God wanted me to share my life, He would need to work things out. Jill would need to find herself spiritually, without a romantic entanglement pressuring her to make a decision that was not really her own. The way one chooses to walk—with God, or away from God—must be an individual decision. Marriage may help or hinder but should not dictate this choice, or priorities get mixed up. Marriage must be built on the foundation of a relationship with God in order to stand strong in the winds of life. Marriage, in itself, is not big enough, important enough, or strong enough to be the foundation of a relationship with God.

Distance seemed at the time to provide a truce in my personal war between romance and reason! I buried myself in my coursework—and prayed.

My mom's call that Sunday morning with the news that Jill had been baptized was like the blast of a thousand trumpets, with the walls of Jericho falling. Suddenly there were no barriers between us, and I eagerly looked forward to Christmas vacation with Jill.

I never asked Jill to be my wife. She had always presumed we would get married, so when the barrier of being unequally yoked crumbled, my personal war was over, and we announced our engagement.

We were married on September 2, 1973. Little did I realize that religious persuasion was only a small part of the compatibility equation in marriage. I had presumed that by belonging to the same church we would be equally yoked. Oh, how wrong I was!

(Jill) The announcement of our engagement may have been the end of Allan's quest, but for me it was just the beginning. I guess I just loved the challenge of the chase. Setting a goal and going after it was an exhilarating experience. It always had been. Like a game of chess, I enjoyed planning my moves and watching how my opponent responded. But when the game was over and my options played out, I was confused. Is this what I really wanted?

While Allan now had his family firmly backing our decision for marriage, I experienced the opposite. I felt I had no family support. My parents were totally involved in their own issues: the divorce becoming final, financial difficulties, having to sell the family home, Mom and Dad each dating others, and then remarrying within a few months. Where Mom had been so supportive before, she now didn't have the psychological energy necessary to affirm to me that I had made the right decision.

Not only did I feel a lack of support but I was embarrassed about what was happening to my family, which made it difficult for me to confide in others about my situation.

Tradition said that it was the woman's family who planned the wedding. I began to realize that if a wedding was to be planned, I'd have to do it on my own. I felt isolated, detached. Where there should have been family excitement, positive affirmations, planning, and exhilarating anticipation, there was nothing. As a new bride-to-be, I wanted to be the center of attention, but no one seemed to care.

In addition, there was resistance to this new religion and the major lifestyle changes I was suddenly making. I felt a current of family antagonism against my decision. They were concerned that I had been brainwashed. They thought I didn't know what I was doing. Why couldn't I just marry the hometown football captain they all liked and whose family was similar to ours, continue going to the church I had attended all my life, and settle down in our hometown?

3—L.B.L.

Who did I think I was? Was I too good for the rest of the family?

All this led me to question whether I was marrying a college graduate merely to reach my goal of becoming rich and famous. Was this decision my way of climbing the status ladder so I'd have more money and be looked up to, as I had previously climbed the popularity ladder in high school? What were my motives? Did I really love Allan for the person he was—or did I love the idea of marrying Allan so he could rescue me from the disaster my life in Rockwood had become?

I was confused. Was I running ahead of the Lord?

Ever since I had nearly died at six weeks of age, my family had treated me as special. I had taken advantage of this and had always been able to manipulate my folks into letting me do whatever I wanted. Was this merely another one of my manipulation games? I learned early how to use my coquettish actions to get my way. Is this what I had done now? Had I gone too far this time? Would I someday be sorry I had turned against the ways of my family? In trying to reach for a better life, would I in the end lose everything?

To add to my confusion, a number of fellows began to take a special interest in me. Jerry, who attended my former church, was most insistent that I go out with him.

"Just because you're engaged doesn't mean you can't go out to dinner occasionally with friends," he said. "After all, Allan's in California, and you're alone."

Jerry was my brother John's teacher and the basketball coach. We talked when I'd take John to the games. Jerry's persistence won out, and eventually I gave in to going out to dinner with him. He tried to convince me that I never should have changed my religion. He was persuasive, and I found it difficult to argue with his reasoning. I knew I probably shouldn't be going out with him. But I enjoyed once again being the center of someone's attention. He took me to the nicest restaurants and treated me as if I were someone special. At that moment in my life, I needed someone who cared. His friendship and his constant badgering for me to give up this foolish religion and end my engagement only added to my confusion. I decided to end the relationship with Jerry after he parked in the local Baptist church parking lot in full view of the lighted steeple and kept up a constant barrage of accusations and criticism against my newfound faith until one or two in the morning. I began to compare the gentle way in which I had been led to Bible truth in the Adventist church, where I was allowed to make my own decision, to his harsh brainwashing techniques, and I was angry.

After Jerry, a number of other fellows, mostly from work, helped provide transportation for me to get back and forth to swimming lessons and my job. I needed them, since I didn't have a car. But they all sang the same tune. "Give up this foolish religion and your idea of marrying Allan." It was almost as if the devil were trying in every way possible to discourage me in the decision I had made. But in spite of it all, I remained true to what I believed was right and continued to plan for my wedding.

Since my mom had remarried and moved to Cleveland, Tennessee, in May, the Kennedy family, especially Mom

Kennedy, became my major support. Allan completed his graduate studies and returned to Tennessee a few weeks before our wedding. Our time was spent making last-minute arrangements. We could get better acquainted later. I was committed to going through with this, but that didn't ease the stress.

Even on my wedding day, my family was still reeling with tension. My sister, still questioning the wisdom of my religious choice, decided not to attend the ceremony. Deeply hurt, I was hoping to the last moment that she would reconsider and attend. My folks, each one now married to another spouse, were not on speaking terms. I began to wonder if they would even show up. They did—with my dad arriving just in time to walk me down the aisle. It was not the way I would have wanted it. But it was my wedding day.

As I clutched my father's arm, I looked around at the beautifully decorated Presbyterian church filled with friends and family and began my walk toward Allan. As our eyes met, I knew I had made the right decision. We said, "I do," and "until death do us part," and then, during the prayer, I burst into tears. It was not because of regret or sorrow about getting married but rather tears of relief from all the stress of the past months and tears of joy that at last we were together, bound by a lifetime decision that "what God has joined together . . . let no man put asunder." For better—or for worse.

5

Reality Strikes

(Allan) I thought I had done all the preparation necessary for our wedding. I had hidden the car well and had checked the soles of my shoes to make sure no one had written "HELP" on them. But I hadn't anticipated that before I would even have a chance to kiss the bride, she would be in tears! I not only didn't have a tissue for her to wipe them away; I didn't have a clue as to why this was happening on what should have been the happiest day of our lives!

I was soon to learn that marriage is not always romance. As the fog lifted, I began to get the education of my life. I remember some of the "cooking" that came from Jill's kitchen. At times I was tempted to pray, "Lord, save me from this food. Amen"—which was the "blessing" we used to say over the meals served at the school cafeteria. I learned that Jill couldn't match socks, and she hung all the clothes on hangers backward! I also remember the night when I awoke with about half of my body on the bed, one leg hanging off, and Jill sleeping on my back! After unsuccessfully nudging her over several times, I finally got up and went around the bed to get in on the other side. As I started to get in, Jill awakened and asked, "Just what do you think you're doing?" After my meek reply of, "Just going to bed," I was told in no uncertain tones that I could just march right back where I had come from and get in where I belonged!

Another problem Jill had was getting anywhere on time. Several times, out of desperation, I slowly drove off, letting her run to catch up with the car and jump in.

On top of everything else, this girl who, before marriage, had tempted me with her short skirts, sassy eyes, and engaging smile, I discovered afterward, thought sex was a four-letter word. And I had no idea how to change her mind.

All of these things made me question if I had married the right Jill. She was not the girl I thought she was—and marriage surely wasn't the wedded bliss I had anticipated. I felt lonely and disillusioned. I often thought of the comment my Uncle Ralph had made to me before our wedding, "Marriage will be either heaven or hell on earth!" And the way things were going, our marriage was much closer to hell than the heaven I had anticipated. If only Jill would get her life together, act more mature, and show me love and respect, things would be much better.

(Jill) Soon after we were married, Allan's sister gave me a plaque which read: "There are four things a woman should know: How to look like a girl. How to act like a lady. How to think like a man. And how to work like a dog." As the weeks went by, I was certain Allan was the author. I had gotten married for companionship. I wanted to live with someone I could have a good time with. Instead, Allan turned out to be a dictator, always telling me what to do! Not only did Allan prefer to stay home and read when I would rather party but I quickly learned that the housework was all mine. Allan didn't even seem to know how to use a clothes hanger. I may have hung up his clothes backward, as he says, but at least I hung them up! In spite of the fact that it was my job to do the housework, he appeared to know, far better than I, how it should be done, and he did not hesitate to tell me where improvements could be made. I felt that regardless of what I did or how much time I spent on a task, it was never good enough.

After marriage, the surprise love gifts from Allan stopped. He insisted we had to be practical. Somehow I hoped Christmas would be different. We went out and cut a tree together and decorated it with popcorn. When a package for me never appeared under the tree, I wondered what special surprise gift Allan had planned for his new bride. But when Christmas came and went without a gift, I was devastated. He gave me nothing, explaining that he was going to get me something a couple days after Christmas when the sales were on. I had tried to be practical so had purchased a shovel for him—*but at least it was a gift*. When I found he didn't have a present for me, I was so angry I felt like using the shovel on him!

Our first home was close to my ideal: an apartment in a two-story colonial brick house with white pillars, furnished with beautiful antiques. I loved it. Allan, who was an assistant administrator of Woods Memorial Hospital in Etowah, could come home every day for lunch. I could walk to town and visit with all the storekeepers, and once more my social life began to climb as I became involved in various community clubs. The more Allan worked, the more I became involved in my own life. I wanted to go back to school, but Allan, instead of being supportive and helping me figure out a way I could get there, merely said he needed the car. So I gave up the idea—a decision I often regretted. Instead, I became more and more involved in church activities and community projects. I became the hospital auxiliary president, the East Tennessee District president, worked in medical records, and won best decoration at the local garden club.

Because we were located on the main north-south thoroughfare, Allan's Uncle Walt, who had married us, and his wife, Aunt P.K., would often stop to visit and pray with us. Since Allan worked, I was often the only one home. One day I was so miserable because of the way Allan was treating me that I said I didn't feel like praying. I'll never forget Aunt P.K.'s words: "When you don't feel like praying is when you need to pray most." Those words became a guiding force in my budding spiritual life.

Uncle Walt and Aunt P.K. always seemed to show up when our relationship was in the pits. Whether they perceived this or not, I don't know, but I do know their prayers for us kept us going, and Uncle Walt's words "Remember to be kind to each other" would ring in our ears when we were acting like bitter enemies.

During that first year of marriage, I could see our relationship slipping from bad to worse, but I didn't seem to know what to do about it. I longed for Allan's approval, but no matter what I did, nothing ever seemed to be good enough. He thought he was encouraging me to learn new skills when he told me that if I wanted new clothes I could make them myself. I did, but he rarely complimented me. I resented having to do things merely to gain his approval. I knew he valued a nice home and good food, so I became "Miss Homemaker," not because I enjoyed doing these things but to keep him from yelling at me. I started baking bread, and when I knew he was coming home, I'd clean things up. I was doing things to keep him happy, not out of love, but out of a survival mode so I wouldn't be criticized.

The biggest part of my disillusionment had to do with the way Allan lived his religion, or more precisely, the way he didn't! Wasn't a Christian supposed to be kind and gentle at home? Instead, he was critical, harsh, and opinionated, especially when I didn't agree with him. As long as I went along with what he wanted, things were fine. But when he didn't like what I said or did, I could expect a verbal lashing. As our disrespect for each other grew, he would even lash out at me in public, which was devastating. It embarrassed me, because I wanted others to think I had made a good decision to marry such a wonderful Christian gentleman. Instead, I was humiliated. I grew to fear Allan's painful words and would retreat, with a "holier-than-thou" attitude. I had no idea that he was reacting out of frustration because his basic needs as a husband for a satisfying sexual relationship and for respect were not being met.

I loved sharing my faith by going door-to-door and giving out literature and expected that every good Christian should do these things. Allan, however, wasn't interested. Years later, I realized that he was not a people person as I was and that new contacts were painful for him. But I began to question whether his religion was really genuine or not and in the process became resentful and disrespectful. I began to feel like a martyr. I knew I had found Bible truth and tried so hard to live by the standards I felt were right that I became self-righteous and critical. I would say, "You were brought up a good Christian. Why don't you act like it?"

I began to wonder, is this what marriage is all about? I felt like a daughter, married to a demanding father. There was little sharing and little caring. And because of our relationship, I became the rebellious child who talked back and pouted. We had no idea what a man or a woman needed. I needed nurturing and emotional support, but Allan was goal-oriented and after winning me, his next conquest was to find a place to live in the country.

(Allan) Even our definitions of things differed. Take, for example, country living. During our courtship, I had told Jill that I really wanted to live out in the country where we could have some privacy. I meant *ouuuuut* in the country, miles away from any civilization. She didn't object, thinking country living meant being a couple of miles out of town on a paved road surrounded by neighbors. She made it a point to inform me that her dream was to live in a two-story colonial brick house with white pillars, a maid, and a Monte Carlo sitting out front. Sure, I'll admit, at a weak moment I agreed to everything—even the Monte Carlo. But now that we were married, that wasn't really practical. So even though in Jill's mind we were already living in our ideal two-story colonial brick home with white pillars surrounded by people (even if it was a rented apartment), I began to look for remote country property on which to settle. Looking back, even though I tore Jill from her meaningful life in town, our mutual quest for country property and subsequent conquest of it gave us something to focus on outside our own disillusionment about our marriage and the divergent paths our lives were taking.

6

Country Living

(**Allan**) I determined that my next goal in life would be to find a remote place in the country where I could have my privacy. I had spent one year in densely populated southern California, and I hated living on top of people. Now was my chance to escape! After much discussion, Jill seemed open to the idea—but for a far different reason than mine. Convinced the Lord was coming soon, she wanted a place in the country where we could survive the time of trouble. Little did we realize that in the next few years we would both be trying to survive our own time of trouble.

I purchased topographical maps of a large part of southeastern Tennessee, scrutinizing every possible piece of land for sale within twenty miles east of the little town of Etowah in the foothills of the Smokies. We began scouting out the area.

One day, following our maps, I decided that we should go west along the north side of the Hiwassee River from Reliance to Spring Town to see if any property was available. When we came to Spring Creek, Jill, a reluctant swimmer who is fearful of deep water, was sure the water was too deep to cross. After surveying the water from the bank, I decided that if we went slowly, we could proceed. Inching down into the water, "Old Blue" was making good progress until I heard the fan blades hitting water. Moments later, the motor quit. In a panic, Jill tried in vain to open the door against the weight of the flowing water so she could get out.

As the water equalized at the level of our seats, we were able to open a door and wade to the bank. Having noticed a farm just before the creek, we went there to ask if they had a tractor to pull us out. The lady who answered the door said, "Y'all are stuck in the creek!"

Jill asked, "How did you know?"

She replied, "Well, honey, you're wet clear up to your waist!"

We pulled the car out, and miraculously it started, even though water came out of the exhaust! I'm sure we were quite a sight heading back down the river road, opening doors as we went around curves to let the water out! To my surprise and embarrassment, Jill loved the adventure. She must have been biting her tongue to keep from saying, "I told you so."

Some months later, we saw an advertisement that

sounded interesting for sixty-six acres in a remote area only eight miles from the hospital. I went into the real-estate office to inquire. While the agent was getting a map of the property and preparing the 4 x 4 Bronco for the trek to the country, the owner of the agency said, "He won't want that. It's too far out. Nobody can get into that place. It would be too much work to make anything out of it."

As soon as I heard these words, I was sure this place was exactly what I was looking for.

(Jill) It was Friday afternoon, freezing cold, and threatening snow. Allan had left work early and had stopped by the real-estate office to inquire about the sixty-six acres of property he had seen advertised in the paper. I was feeling miserable with the flu and was wrapped up in a quilt, sipping hot mint tea in our warm, cozy apartment when Allan came in stamping his wet feet on the entry rug. He yelled in an excited voice, "Jill, come quick. Get ready. We've got to go. There's this incredible place in the country that we've just got to check out."

I sighed. The last thing I wanted to do was leave my cozy little apartment and head up into the wilderness, especially on a day like this—and when I was not feeling good. But Allan's excitement was contagious, and after moaning and groaning a few minutes, I got myself dressed in long johns, parka, and mittens and headed out to who knows where.

We drove and drove and drove, forded a stream, and continued driving. It was the longest eight miles I have ever experienced. Finally, there were so many fallen trees— along with brush and briars growing higher than our heads—that we left the Bronco and set out on foot. By now the snow was beginning to fall. It was dreary and desolate, and as we walked up the valley, it seemed that the mountains, or knobs, as they are called, were closing in on me. I felt smothered. Did Allan really want this place? The whole thing seemed impossible. But the more depressing it became to me, the more Allan's enthusiasm mounted. In the end I said Yes, for I did want him to have his dream.

It was 1974, but it might as well have been in the 1800s, for we were true pioneers trying to establish a homestead with very little money, no equipment other than an ancient chainsaw, and the sweat of our brows. We basically chopped, cut, and sawed our way into our property, re-establishing the old logging road that had been crude even in its day. Finally, on days when the creek was low enough, we could drive "Old Blue" into the valley, where we began to make a home for ourselves.

First came the beehives. Allan was intent on becoming self-sufficient—and every home needs honey, right? Allan bought a couple of hives and put them on the property and later purchased another eighteen from a place in Alabama. He'd told me that bees don't like thunder, but what do you do when a stormy day is the only one you have on which to work the hives? So, ignoring reality, Allan and I drove up to the hives with the thunder rumbling in the background. Allan got on his beekeeping gear while I sat in the car with a good book. A few minutes later, I saw Allan running down the hill toward the car with a swarm of bees behind him. I rolled up the windows, locked the doors, and anxiously watched him pass the car and continue running on down the road until he and the bees disappeared. Fifteen minutes later, after the bees had dispersed, Allan came trudging back up the road. I laughed all the way home. He still doesn't think it was funny.

Next came the goats to eat the undergrowth and keep the place cleaned up. I had never had animals around, so it was quite an experience. I remember filling the feed bucket with grain and heading out to feed the goats for the first time. I couldn't believe it. They charged me. So I ran, with the bucket swinging by my side as I tried to race to safety. Allan heard my screams for help, saw the goats stampeding behind me, and yelled, "Set the bucket down." It hadn't occurred to me that the goats wanted the food and not just to chase me! I set it down and was relieved that the solution was so simple!

I hate snakes. And this place was said to be filled with them. But I questioned that, because in all our chopping and clearing, I hadn't seen any. Allan told me to never pick up stones before kicking them over to check for snakes, but I had grown careless—until the day I kicked over a stone with a poisonous copperhead underneath. After that, I took more seriously the stories the old-timers told me about life in the boonies.

Our goal was to get into our own home as soon as possible, with as little cost as possible. Dad Kennedy suggested a mobile home. I went down to South Carolina, and he and I went shopping for something we could afford. Unfortunately, something we could afford wasn't exactly habitable. We ended up purchasing a 10 x 50 *well-used* fix-up unit and had it transported to our place. Getting it from the road to the selected location on our land was a major task. We blasted rocks, cut trees, and arranged for a crawler to pull the mobile home over the creek and on into our wilderness valley. It wasn't exactly the two-story colonial brick home with white pillars that I had become accustomed to living in, but it was ours. We repaired, sanded, and varnished the walls, painted, and recarpeted. Originally we thought we might be a month or two without electricity, which I thought I could handle. Then we learned we needed a septic system before the electricity could be installed. Allan put one in immediately. But when the electric company representatives came to inspect the location after the septic system was installed, the price was exorbitant, because our dwelling was considered temporary. So there went the idea of electric lights, appliances, indoor bathroom facilities, and running water! Allan always made it a point to tell people we had running water, "as long as Jill runs to the creek to get it." With this new development, getting an outhouse became an immediate priority.

A friend had property with an old doorless two-holer outhouse on it that wasn't being used, and he said we could have it if we'd haul it away. We took the old logging truck Allan had purchased and headed off to bring it home. We finally got the thing on the truck and tied it down. But Allan was still afraid the wind would blow it over. I volunteered to sit inside to hold it down, so we headed down the highway with me perched on the throne waving to those who gawked! Allan almost died of embarrassment, but I reveled in the attention. The outhouse served its purpose, even though we never got around to getting a door on it.

4—L.B.L.

I really didn't like the idea of this primitive existence, but I knew Allan was trying to develop this property without going into debt, and for a few months I figured I could enjoy the adventure of camping out. I just accepted it as another challenge in life.

We immediately began preparations to build a permanent dwelling, felling trees, hauling them to the mill to be sawed into boards, and drawing plans. The barn came first, then the chicken house, then four years later, the house—not exactly my two-story colonial style brick home with the white pillars, but a cozy country home. And with it, electricity! Ah, the joy of finally being able to bathe in a hot tub rather than a cold creek!

The four years without electricity were quite an experience, to say the least. About a mile from our trailer was a secluded spring-fed creek, which we adopted as our bathtub. The water was frigid, but I got used to it. I never did get used to bathing naked out in the open though! I was afraid someone would come by, so I always wore my bathing suit, much to the amusement of Allan. When the creek got too cold, we carried water from the spring to our trailer and heated it in a teapot on the wood stove. Allan got pretty proficient at bathing in a gallon of water on our front porch.

For heat, we had an Ashley wood stove that we set up in our living room, with a smokestack sticking out the window. It worked great until the wind blew the wrong way, blowing the smoke back down the stack and into the trailer. We'd then have to open all the windows to clear the smoke out, button up our jackets, and put on earmuffs until the house heated once again.

To keep things refrigerated, the folks gave us a big ice chest. We used that in the summer, but once the weather was cold enough, we simply set our food outside the door, hoping wild animals wouldn't help themselves.

When we bought the property, I had asked, "What do you do when the creek rises?" The answer was, "You don't go home." After a couple of years of fording the stream and many days of not being able to get home because the water was too high, Allan finally decided we needed a bridge. It consisted of two trees for each track across the creek, with boards nailed over them, just wide enough for the tires to cross. I called it our "hit or miss" bridge. There was no room for error. I got pretty good at hitting it but always worried that one false move and I would be dumped into the stream. We used the bridge like that for a couple of years until a neighbor suggested that we get oak boards to span the entire width. Having a *real* bridge meant a lot to me. It was insurance that I could get in or out regardless of the weather. After the project was completed, we used the bridge for several years. One day I noticed it leaning slightly and creaking as I crossed, so I began fording the stream again. Because going through all that water was hard on the brakes, Allan asked me why I was doing that when we had a perfectly good bridge! When I complained about the leaning and creaking, he assured me and said, "There is nothing wrong with that bridge. It's not going to fall." But in spite of his insistence, I simply refused to drive if it meant crossing the bridge. One afternoon, Allan was going to town for something, and I asked him if he would take me to the grocery store. All of a sudden, just as he drove the car onto the bridge, there was a loud cracking sound, and the right side of the bridge collapsed, plunging the car on its side into the creek. When I finally managed to crawl out, Allan yelled, "Run to the house for the truck and chain saw." Before driving back with the chain saw, I phoned an SOS to our neighbors, yelling, "The bridge collapsed." They must have thought we had been injured, for by the time I returned to the scene of the accident, they were racing down the road to our rescue. So much for a bridge and easy access to civilization. Now it was back to fording the stream once again.

One of the scariest moments we had in that trailer was being awakened by a deep, slow, forceful panting sound that penetrated the whole valley. The first time it happened I was so petrified I couldn't speak. Allan and I just lay still in bed listening. After a while, the panting subsided, and I tried to sleep. The next day we went out to see what it could have been, but there was nothing unusual. Yet night after night, the terrifying breathing sound returned. I began to wonder if our valley was inhabited by demons. The whole experience was unnerving.

One night I awoke again to the sound and reached for Allan, only to find the bed empty. I grabbed for my flashlight. It was gone. I got up and groped my way through the dark and found the back door wide open. I quickly shut and locked it, and shaking with fright, went back to the bedroom to peer through the window. I could see a flashlight bobbing up and down in the valley and figured it was Allan.

Fifteen minutes later, Allan was banging on the door. I

opened it and was shocked to see him standing there with only his tennis shoes on and his rifle in hand. He told the story of hearing the noise, jumping up, grabbing his rifle determined to shoot whatever it was, and dashing outside. Our Saint Bernard, Bruno, raced ahead about thirty feet, whipped around, and returned with his tail between his legs. Allan ran in that direction but never saw anything. After that incident, the sound never returned. Later, an old-timer told Allan that it was a bear "barking" at the dog, trying to get the dog to chase it.

A year after we moved into the trailer, I told Allan I could live without electricity but not without a phone. I had to be able to talk to someone other than the four walls and God! (Sorry, no offense, Lord! It's my sanguine personality!) This was no little task, since a trench two feet deep had to be dug across the steep hill and through the dense woods for about eighteen hundred feet. Allan rented a ditch witch. It was so steep coming down the hill that we had to loop a cable around the machine's axle and wrap it around a tree to let the machine dig its way down the hill without rolling end over end. With the ditch dug, knights in shining armor (the phone company's installation crew) laid the cable and hooked up my link to the outside world.

When I finally got pregnant and was thinking ahead to the final hours when I'd be counting the minutes between contractions, I was thankful that at last we had a phone. Just a year and a half before, and two months pregnant, I had begun to cramp and was bleeding slightly. Because of the weather, we couldn't ford the creek so had to leave our car out on the road. Our Willys Jeep was frozen to the ground, with three or four inches of snow around it, and the snow was still falling. There was no phone to relieve my anxiety, so I went to bed and hoped things would get better. When the contractions intensified and the bleeding increased, Allan decided we could wait no longer and walked the mile and a quarter to the nearest neighbors, the Lethcos, to call the doctor. As I lay there alone in the pitch black stillness of the night with only the flicker of the kerosene lamp, I began to pray as I had never prayed before. I wanted so badly to have a child—a son for Allan. After all, he had wanted a dozen, and I had already had one miscarriage. Forty minutes later, he tramped into the trailer with the news that if certain conditions developed, I would need to go to the hospital immediately. Unfortunately, I was by then experiencing those very conditions.

Allan quickly turned around and hiked back to the same neighbors to call the hospital and inform them that he was bringing me in to the hospital. Mr. Lethco, overhearing enough of the conversation to realize our dilemma, offered to drive his pickup truck up to our place and bring us out to where our car was parked near their home. As I lay there in the dark trailer praying, the sound of Lethco's truck was music to my ears. Help had arrived.

I had lost that first baby. Now I didn't want to lose another. At seven months, when false labor started, I had been told to quit work and get off my feet. During the last two months, my anticipation—as well as my anxiety—heightened. I don't think I could have survived the loss of another baby and was thankful that at least this time we had a phone in case I needed help. Wednesday morning, just a couple days before my due date, we awoke to the worst situation I could imagine—our phone was out of order. We could receive calls but could not call out. Allan assured me that he would report this to the phone company the first thing when he got to work so it could be fixed immediately. After he notified the phone company, he called me, saying that the repairman would be there right away and that I should call him if I should start labor. I waited and waited. No repairman. The afternoon wore on. I was frantic when I realized that Allan was in meetings and had no idea that our phone was still out of service. What if my labor were to start?

Finally, at five o'clock when I heard him coming, I got out of bed for the first time that day and sat on the couch. As he walked in the door, my water broke. With no phone to report the progress of my labor to determine when we should leave for the sixty-mile drive to the hospital in Knoxville, we went to town immediately and used a pay phone to call the doctor. He suggested we wait and not come until the contractions started on a regular basis. There was no way I was going back to our trailer without a phone, so we went to the home of friends who had been through childbirth three times. They assured me that I should take a hot shower and relax on the sofa, and that everything was progressing normally.

Four hours later, we left for the hospital. Jeremy was born the next day, May 18, 1978. But it wasn't as we had planned. We'd taken all the Lamaze classes, driving sixty miles up to Knoxville every week, and we were looking forward to this experience to help bond our fragmenting family. And wouldn't you know it, the old disgruntled doctor neither of us liked was the one on call. He never communicated anything to prepare us for what might happen if for some reason I could not have a vaginal delivery. All I remember is that when he checked the monitor, he yelled, "Stat. Section. Baby's endangered!"—and they whisked me away to surgery. Allan was angry to be excluded without any consultation. I was afraid. In the rush to administer the spinal, they injected it too high, and it felt as if I couldn't breathe. I was able to whisper to the anesthesiologist, "I can't breathe," and he said, "Don't worry, I'll breathe for you." But I was sure I was going to die. Thus we began our parenting adventure.

7

Parenting—Life in the War Zone

(Jill) A week later, with our firstborn son in my arms, I returned to our little 10- by 50-foot trailer with the doctor's words ringing in my ears: "Soak in a hot tub of water for at least fifteen minutes every day." I gulped when he gave me those instructions. It had been years since I had been able to soak in my own hot tub of water. We still had no electricity, and the only running water was in the creek. I looked at the doctor with questioning eyes and said, "I don't know if I can do that, but I'll try." I didn't attempt to explain.

Allan was very supportive of me in my condition and would apply warm towels to my abdomen. But it wasn't quite the warm bath the doctor had ordered.

Mom Kennedy stayed with us for two weeks, and finally Allan's dad talked to him. "Allan, I think it's time, with a young baby, that you get a house built. You and Jill living like this is one thing, but having a newborn and living without running water and electricity is another."

We hadn't built because Allan didn't want to go into debt. But now Allan, taking seriously the responsibility of parenthood, began to make plans to build up on the ridge we had selected. And with the house would come electricity, a bathtub—and eventually, warm water!

We moved into our Tennessee mountaintop home a day before Jeremy's first birthday. I was so thrilled that Thursday night when we had the final inspection I danced around the house flipping the electrical switches on and off.

"Lights! Lights!" I shouted. "How wonderful to have lights!"

Allan used to say, "It's really easy to please a woman. Just live without electricity for four years, and she'll be happy with anything!" And he was just about right! This house, built by our own hard labor—mostly Allan's—was a dream come true.

But I wasn't the only one who seemed awed by the wonder of it all. Jeremy, just barely walking, toddled around the large, empty living room. After he had learned to walk in a 10- by 50-foot mobile home, it was like going from a corral to a pasture. I've seen those frisky colts kick up their heels with the sheer ecstasy of enjoying plenty of space. Although Jeremy didn't exactly kick up his heels, he seemed to revel in the freedom of the extra space and ran from one place to another.

Friday afternoon all the relatives came, bringing a U-Haul truck loaded with heirlooms from Grandma's house, and by sundown the whole house was furnished. I have to hand it to Allan's mother. She had a floor plan of our house, and she had drawn out the exact place where every piece of furniture was to be placed.

But as wonderful as the house was, there was one thing missing—the water was not yet connected. So after moving in, I still had to bathe in the creek. And can you believe it, for the first time in four years, that Friday afternoon as I bathed in that cold creek, a snake slithered between my feet? I screamed, ran to the car, and drove up the drive to the safety of my brand-new house. There I finished rinsing my hair over the edge of the front porch, using a jug of water. I remember thinking how glad I was that we would soon have running water in the house. If I had known it would be another two months, I might have sat down and cried. At that moment, sixty more days of bathing in a "snake-infested" creek would have been more than I could handle. But God knows how much we can take, and He mercifully spared me that knowledge.

If you've ever tried to build a house yourself, you know the time it takes, so it's easy to see why, during the first year after Jeremy's birth, neither Allan nor I had much time to think of anything else. Add to this equation a colicky newborn baby who literally demanded to be held or attended to full time, and you can understand why Allan and I never really had time to discuss childrearing. We never talked about parenting styles and their possible outcomes. Our main focus was on how to get Jeremy to stop crying, feeding him on the strict four-hour schedule Allan's mother had set up for us, carrying in water for his bath and heat-ing it, and diapering and dressing him. We were still living in a survival mode, coping moment by moment.

(Allan) My routine that first year was to come home to our trailer, eat supper, and then immediately go across the valley and up the hill to the construction site, where I'd work on our house until midnight or one o'clock, then come back home, fall into bed, and leave the next morning just in time to make it to work. Every Sunday was spent building. So really, that first year or so, I was so busy building that I didn't really have time to discuss parenting with Jill. She was basically a good mother. I might have done some things differently, but I didn't interfere—I just didn't have time. I figured that when Jeremy was older and not so dependent on his mother, I'd get more involved with his training.

But it's unfair to say I wasn't involved in parenting. I did my fatherly thing with my son, such as taking him on his first tractor ride. He must have been about five months old. We had an old Ferguson tractor, which served a dual purpose. It not only powered itself along but it blew out blue smoke in the back to fog the mosquitoes. Jill nearly panicked. There was probably good reason for her fear, because she knew that I had rolled a tractor before, and she was terrified that I would roll the tractor with her precious child on it.

Then there were the times Jeremy's crying became so prolonged and intense that finally Jill would say, "I can't take it anymore." So I'd take Jeremy outside, and he'd watch the dog and the birds, and all of a sudden he'd burp real big, and everything would be fine. Jill always said I had the magic touch. I just didn't use it often enough!

Jill has always had dozens of projects going, none very productive income-wise, but they have kept her busy. One of the jobs she continued to do after Jeremy was born was to be the Southeast Tennessee Regional Auxiliary representative for the Tennessee Hospital Association, which included running district meetings and attending state board meetings. Jill enjoyed taking Jeremy along with her, so she very rarely got a babysitter.

(Jill) Just before Jeremy's first birthday, I was attending an auxiliary board meeting and had Jeremy and a teenaged helper with me. Since I was still nursing Jeremy, I took a break to feed him. He was nursing and began playfully biting me. I thought it must be about time to wean him, but I wasn't very educated on how to go about doing this. All I knew was that the biting hurt and I needed to stop it.

I said to Jeremy, "No, Jeremy, don't bite Mommy!" in a tone of voice that said, "I mean it!" He continued biting, watching me closely. He knew what he was doing and totally ignored what I had said. I repeated, "No, Jeremy, don't bite!" When he continued, I took my finger and snapped his chin. He looked at me in surprise, let go of my breast, and never again would nurse. A few hours later, I tried to get him to nurse, because my breasts were becoming engorged. He refused! I was miserable. I tried pumping them to relieve the pressure and finally had to go to the doctor to get shots. That's the first major indication we had about the strength of the will in our firstborn. When he made a decision, he would stick with it, even if it meant going hungry!

(Allan) Jill was very protective when it came to the

children's health or safety. She would fly into a fury if someone offered them something with sugar in it. At times I
thought she was overly protective and tried to cushion them
from experiences that boys needed in order to test their
wings, gain confidence, and learn new skills. "Be careful.
Don't get hurt!" were her watchwords. I wanted them to
be tough and allowed them more freedom to learn from
their mistakes.

(**Jill**) I'll admit I may have been too protective. But let
me tell you, after having three miscarriages and enduring
two C-sections, when I was sure I was going to die, my
two boys were very precious to me. I wasn't about to have
anything happen to them through my neglect or by allow-
ing them to do something foolish.

(**Allan**) Jill and I had minor disagreements those first
few years, but our arguments increased significantly when
Jonathan came along. It probably had more to do with
Jeremy's age—by then he was a strong-willed, inquisitive
"terrible two"—than merely the fact that we had two children. The reason our conflict over child rearing escalated
was because Jill and I had two diametrically opposed ideas
of what childhood should consist of. I was of the opinion
that we should train up our children in the way that we
thought they should go, and she thought childhood was
the season of magic, play, wonder, and fun. The more I
pushed for things to go my way, the more determined Jill
was to have hers.

(**Jill**) I grew up as a happy, fun-loving, carefree kid who
enjoyed climbing trees and playing hide-and-seek. That's
what I wanted for our children. I wanted them to be re-

sponsible, but I also wanted them to have time to enjoy their growing-up years. I wanted them to have time to play. If they could be happy, obedient, and love God, I would have reached my ultimate goal as a successful parent.

Unfortunately, Allan's idea was to train our boys to be tough, industrious, and organized—to carry responsibility and use their heads. And his method of achieving this was to have them work, work, work! That's why, when they were little, we bought chickens for them so they could start an egg distribution business and raised Australian Shepherd dogs and Christmas trees. At times Allan expected the boys to do things that I didn't think they were mature enough to do, and this would cause major conflict as each of us would try to balance out what we considered the extremes of the other.

(Allan) I demanded obedience—Jill coaxed it out of the boys. If I told them to be quiet in church, they knew they didn't have much choice. But I could see they took advantage of Jill by pushing the limits when she was around. It was tough for me to understand why Jill couldn't see the wisdom of my ways.

(Jill) This is a typical scene from "A Day in the Life of the Kennedys." Allan would come home from work, and invariably, since the boys and I had been having fun hiking, baking bread, giving Bible studies, or helping our neighbors, something important on his list wouldn't get done. As far as Allan was concerned, there was no reason not to have accomplished the tasks that he had determined we should have completed while he was away. Our reason for not doing something, which seemed so legitimate to me, was treated as an irresponsible excuse by Allan.

He would say, "You're the adult. What's wrong with you? Why can't you get these things done? And why didn't you use your head?"

I tried to cushion the blows and quiet him down with my coquettish way. It had worked when we first were courting, but it was counterproductive now. His response was, "Jill, when are you going to grow up!"

(Allan) My parenting style quickly adopted the life commandments that had been handed down to me by my parents.

The first commandment was, "Cleanliness is next to godliness, and neatness is a close second."

My home had been very conservative. My mother was a schoolteacher; therefore, we had lists. One of the earliest things I remember was a wall chart my mother had made with pictures of things we had to do. We were taught to be organized. Everything had a place, and we were expected to keep it in that place. If we didn't, Mom had a grab bag and anything found lying around would be confiscated and put into the bag. Eventually, we would remember that we wanted the item and wonder where it had gone. More than likely it was in the grab bag, and in order to redeem it, we would have to pay anywhere from a nickel to a quarter, depending on the relative size and value of the item. Needless to say, purchasing back our own things quickly taught us to be responsible and to keep our belongings in their place. One thing I was certain about—I didn't want my children growing up to be like their mother, who left things all over the house. On numerous occasions I was tempted to resurrect the grab bag to train Jill, but I restrained myself, vowing that I would implement this system when my boys were old enough to benefit from this training. Actually, we never did this with our children, basically because I wasn't home long enough to make the system work and Jill would probably have thought this close to child abuse.

(Jill) In contrast to Allan's childhood, when I was growing up, I faithfully cleaned my room every three months or so, or more often if I would smell something like the dead dissected fish from biology class that I had forgotten to throw out. It wasn't as if my mom hadn't tried to train me to do housework—she was always on my case. But I far preferred to be out delivering papers with my dad on our paper route while my sister was corralled into doing housework. Mom finally found a job I liked—taking our laundry to the laundromat every Saturday morning with my dad. And once I started driving, I enjoyed doing the grocery shopping. As long as there were people to talk with, which made the job fun, I didn't mind work.

(Allan) The second commandment my parents handed down to me was "Better not go at all than arrive late." The net result of this was a miserable time every Sabbath morning with Jill and the boys, as I berated them for their lack of responsibility in not being ready to leave for church on time. The most simple solution for me as the father—managing the dressing of the boys—never occurred to me. I guess it was probably because I never had seen my father in this role that I figured this was a woman's work. Mom somehow managed to be organized enough to see that all four of us were ready to go in plenty of time when we

5—L.B.L.

needed to go. It was not until the boys were in school that light began to dawn, and I took over the supervision of Sabbath-morning preparation. I'd get up in plenty of time, get the boys organized, and when I'd tell them what I expected, they did it. Many times the three of us were ready before Jill.

The third commandment I parented by was "If you want to eat, you've got to work." This was the rule of our family, and it tempered everything we did. Work was just a part of life. We never considered the possibility that there was any other option.

While Jill grew up with Easter egg hunts and bunnies, trick-or-treating with bags full of candy, a community Santa Claus who came to her house where she could sit on his knee and ask for toys, and even got money under her pillow from the tooth fairy, I had none of this nonsense during my childhood. Our family system was based on the work ethic. You had to work for everything you got. None of this free stuff.

While Jill went to Vacation Bible School to have fun, I went to help with the program. While I was out cultivating the cornfield with the horse, Jill was out playing left field. While Jill's family vacationed at Cumberland Mountain State Park or Lake Winnepasauka or went to the circus or state fair for entertainment, our family went to Washington, D.C. to visit the relatives, or we went to camp meeting. There was always a purpose behind the trip we took, above and beyond mere enjoyment. I had learned that in life there were no free handouts and I was going to make sure my children learned that fact well.

(Jill) Allan's representation of his childhood turned me off, because he came across as so demanding—as if this were the only way to raise children. Even though there was a lot of good in it, I resented it when he pushed his way on me, and I determined I would not raise my children to have such a stark outlook on life as their father had. I wanted their childhood to be more positive, without so many demands and words of criticism. I was going to enjoy life with the boys, and, consequently, that didn't always include Allan, because he was such a stick in the mud!

On the other hand, Allan saw the way I had grown up as utterly useless. What good did tooth fairies and Santa Clauses do to help a child grow up to be productive and useful for society? Growing up the way I did was to Allan a waste of time.

As we tried to see the other's point of view, I decided I should at least read a book that my church had published about how to have a Christian family. I ended up underlining everything about how a father should behave, rather than seeing areas where I needed improvement. Allan was so forceful and overpowering that I could only see the faults in him and never considered the faults in my own parenting style.

Eventually, however, God led us to a more balanced approach to child rearing. I began to realize there was a lot of good in what Allan wanted for the children, as long as it wasn't carried to an extreme. I determined to help the boys be more orderly, to try harder to be on time, and for them to be responsible in carrying out age-appropriate tasks. I even copied Allan's mother's idea and made a chart with drawings of chickens, a bucket with eggs, a bed, and a broom to remind the boys of their daily tasks—and I rewarded them with smiley faces. By the time I was home-schooling both boys, their rooms were inspected before breakfast, they would prepare a hot meal for lunch, and they took responsibility for the care of the animals without my having to remind them.

(Allan) As Jill began to appreciate my parenting style more, I also realized what a blessing it was that Jill was committed to be home with the boys. When Jeremy was born, even though she liked associating with people so much, Jill quit working part time doing medical records in order to be home with him. I was pleased that Jill enjoyed the boys so much that we seldom had babysitters, and when it came time for schooling, Jill chose to home-school.

But even though we eventually mellowed and began to appreciate the parenting styles each of us brought to this family, the years when the boys were little were filled with major disagreements. These were usually lengthy, heated, verbal exchanges that never solved anything except to get us both to the point that we could hardly stand each other. To top it off, these exchanges were often in front of the boys. Finally, one of us would declare that we couldn't and wouldn't stand it any longer and that we were leaving, but that we were going to take the boys. And then we both dug in our stubborn heels, because both of us were determined the boys were "going with me"! And that's where it always ended.

For a long time we didn't recognize that our disagreements had any impact on the boys, but after several years of this, even I had to admit that Jeremy was really acting smart, sassy, and disrespectful to Jill. For a number of years I was blind to the fact that he was merely reflecting the way I treated Jill. Since Jonathan was younger, he didn't seem to be affected as much, but Jeremy sometimes showed open disrespect for his mother, and I'll admit that some of the things he said in public were very embarrassing.

As Jill and I began pulling together more evenly in our marriage harness (see chapter 11), parenting seemed to come easier also. We began to discuss problem areas and strategies for dealing with them and to compromise more. Obviously, since I had caused the respect problem, I was the one who needed to address its correction. Personally, it would have been easier if I had merely started correcting Jeremy for his disrespectful words and actions, without worrying about my own behavior. However, I decided that to be effective with Jeremy, I had first to change my own behavior. This became a special project for me, and eventually his attitude came around, so that he showed respect not only to his mother but to women in general. I'm just thankful that he was still teachable and that this behavior was caught and corrected before it was too late.

(Jill) One of the things Allan and I agreed upon in our parenting was the value of religion for our family. We truly believed that "Unless the Lord builds the house, they labor in vain who build it" (Psalm 127:1, NKJV).

Church was a very important part of our lives. Weekly, we went to Sabbath services, and from the time our children were a few months old until they were ten and graduated into the junior division, I was involved in teaching, leading out, or playing the piano in their Sabbath School classes. When the boys graduated into the junior division, Allan became much more involved in their Sabbath School classes.

We also had regular morning and evening worship times with our boys, even if moments before or after we ourselves were involved in a major argument. I sometimes wondered what good our worship times were doing for Allan and me, but I never doubted the value of this regular time with God for our children. Now I'm happy we did have worships, because I've learned that research studies are finding that children who have daily devotional times in their families are more eager to follow the spiritual and moral values of their parents. I know there are no 100 percent guarantees when you're raising children, but it makes me feel good that we've done something right.

Now that our boys are getting close to the age of emancipation and our parenting is less intense on a minute-by-minute basis, I look back in awe that God brought us through the war zone and has given us all, including the boys, such healthy views about life.

(Allan) Perhaps the story that best illustrates how God can help you through tough times with your children happened when I asked Jonathan, who was about ten years old at the time, to come downstairs for worship. He didn't come, and since I knew my blunt, straightforward manner sometimes bruised Jonathan's sensitive spirit, I asked Jill to please follow up on what I had asked and have him come down.

As Jonathan came down the stairs, he made a disrespectful comment about his mother. That was just at the time I was trying to model respect for Jill, and I was requiring it from the boys, so I said, "You are not going to relate to your mother in that way!"

Jonathan didn't even get to the bottom of the stairs. He became angry and stomped back up the stairs with the comment, "I hate living in this family, and I'm not going to any longer!" He went to his room to pack.

Jill, Jeremy, and I continued to sit in the living room wondering what to do next, and in several minutes Jonathan came down the stairs with his pack on his back. As he started to go out the door, I said to him, "Well, the least you can do is tell your mother goodbye."

"Goodbye," he said flatly—and then he left.

"Allan, you've got to do something," Jill said. "He's going to run away!" But frankly, I didn't know what to do. It was cold and dark outside, and we just sat there for fifteen or twenty minutes. Finally, I got up and went out the front door and sat on the porch steps. Our dog Callahan came over, and I began talking out loud to him.

"Well, Callahan, our family is having a pretty hard time tonight. I love Jonathan, but I can't let him be disrespectful to his mother. If Jonathan doesn't want to stay with our family, maybe you better go and be a companion to him, because he's going to need it."

I sat out there for about another ten minutes, and then I was impressed to pray out loud. I began to pour my heart out to the Lord. I said that I had not meant to be unkind to Jonathan but that as his father I couldn't allow him to be disrespectful to his mother. I told God I appreciated

Jonathan's sensitive spirit and was sorry if I had hurt his feelings. Just as I was saying, "We want Jonathan to come back, but we don't know where he is, so please be with him and protect him," I heard some noise behind me. I ended my prayer with, "Please bring him back safely to us."

All of a sudden, a light from a flashlight shone on the back of my head.

"Oh, Jonathan, is that you?" I asked. Jonathan ran into my arms and said, "Oh, Dad, I'm sorry." I held him for a while, and we talked before going back inside.

The ironic part of the story is that a few nights later, the boys and Jill were playing checkers. Jeremy has an incredibly competitive spirit, and when Jill beat him, he accused her of cheating and pitched a terrible fit, saying, "I don't like y'all anyway, and I'm just going to leave home!"

Suddenly Jonathan began to cry and pleaded with his brother, "Oh, but Jeremy, it is cold and dark out there. You don't want to leave."

The whole mood changed at that moment, and even Jeremy began laughing as we remembered Jonathan's experience. We talked and ended with a prayer that the Lord would help us overcome our weak areas. We often remind the boys, as they see us struggling to be better people, that they don't need to wait until they're our age to start overcoming the negative tendencies they inherited from us.

(Jill) If I could do one thing differently, I would not have held a know-it-all attitude concerning parenting, and I would have read or listened more to the advice that was so readily available through books and seminars—and yes, even through Allan. If I could do it again, I'd pray for more strength to do what was right rather than to let my feelings get in the way and to be so defensive about my parenting style.

Now as I give parenting seminars using Dr. Kay Kuzma's books, I'm often reminded of the camp meeting when I sat in the front row with my preschool-age boys and listened to her words of wisdom. At one point she said, "Too often the conversation in the typical family goes something like this: 'Wake up. Hurry. Get dressed. Eat your breakfast. Hurry. Brush your teeth . . .'" Suddenly Jeremy looked up and said in a loud voice, "Amen!" The audience roared, but I wanted to crawl under the chair. It was hard for me to admit we were so typical and that I didn't know all the answers.

Our dysfunctional marriage relationship heavily impacted our parenting—there is no doubt about that. I now see how vitally important it is, for the sake of your children, to solve your marital problems so that you can pull together when it comes to parenting. The only redeeming factor in our lives was that in spite of all our problems, we gave our children love and gave it abundantly. I cuddled those boys, scratched their backs, read them stories, and played with them before every bedtime. My only regret is that I ignored Allan in the process, secretly rejoicing when he, the "bear," went to bed early, leaving me time to enjoy bedtime alone with the boys.

One more thing. I wish my folks—and Allan's—had been loving in front of us when we were kids, so that we would have had modeled to us the importance of showing affection in front of our children. I regret those lost years when

I spurned Allan's touches and loving gestures. But I'm glad I have learned lessons about love before it was too late—and the boys are now getting some good modeling about how much fun it is to be married. I feel good that we're not only showing affection but that also we're trying to model the importance of solving issues as they arise rather than stuffing them down inside and later reacting with exaggerated and vengeful, negative feelings.

All that is good or bad in a marriage eventually bubbles up and affects one's parenting. Perhaps nothing affected our parenting more than the boundary or control issues that Allan and I struggled with for decades.

CHAPTER

8

Rescuing Allan

(Jill) Not long after we moved into the little 10- by 50-foot trailer in the country, my mother's neighbor, who worked in a hatchery, asked if we would like some chicks that were going to be killed. Allan, having the great humanitarian heart that he does, said we would take them, even though he knew the chicken house was not yet complete. I helped him put a plastic covering on the floor in our tiny living room where the chicks were to stay for a couple weeks until we could get the chicken house ready. But hundreds of peeping voices all day long were too much for me. I thought I would go crazy. So when the floor of the chicken house was completed, we made walls out of Styrofoam blocks, put a tarp over the top, and with a kerosene heater to keep them warm, moved the peeping chicks to their temporary home.

A few days later, when I was home alone and without a phone to call for help, a ferocious windstorm developed. I raced down the path to the chickens only to discover Styrofoam blocks strewn all over the valley, and one melting on the heater. Chicks, dead and alive, were everywhere. I panicked. This was the beginning of my career as a rescue worker—trying to save projects Allan had started. I frantically ran around trying to catch the chicks and to put the Styrofoam blocks back, feeling within me a growing resentment, because I hadn't asked for this trouble. "Why me, Lord?"

(Allan) Jill's accusation was highly unfair. I didn't need to get those chickens. That man had free chickens regularly. We could have gotten them any time. I even asked Jill what she thought about getting the chickens and whether or not we should wait. She said, "It doesn't really matter. I think it will be all right." So I went ahead with the project she had agreed upon. If she would have said, "No," I wouldn't have gotten those chicks. They weren't that important to me.

Then, when the peeping got too much for Jill, I did the best thing I could do to solve the problem by building a makeshift shelter outdoors. I didn't order the wind. It just happened. Yet I was blamed for what happened to the chickens.

(Jill) Wait a minute. I remember that I had said, "It is all right to get the chickens as long as we have a chicken house." But Allan went ahead and got them when all there was to the chicken house was the floor. Besides, I thought this chicken thing was going to be a lot of fun. My experience with chickens was that at Easter I'd get a cute little fuzzy chick. I remember one named Elvis that I got when I was in first grade. It was so darling—it followed me everywhere, even to the outhouse. Elvis was a fun pet. But these chicks were different. They wouldn't shut up and wouldn't stay put!

Plus, I'll admit that it was easier to say Yes to Allan than No. Because Allan was the one working and making money, I felt that if he wanted to get chickens, it was his right, so why should I object as long as he cared for them? But I never said that. The problem was, I never thought about my having to care for those chickens while Allan was at work all day. If only we had communicated better!

Then there were the beehives Allan had purchased in the spring and which by fall were loaded with honey. Helping with the extraction was quite an education. Then what do you do with the honey after it is extracted? Sell it, naturally! If I had wanted another job, I would have gotten another job, but it wouldn't have been extracting and selling honey! Allan never asked if I'd like to make a little extra money in this way. He just expected me to pick up the pieces of whatever he started—and then he got the money, because he managed the family finances.

(Allan) Let me tell you about the honey. I came from a family in which, if one person got a little over his head in a project, the rest of us would help. It wasn't a big deal. I never intended that Jill would have to take over the honey business, but it had been a wonderful year for honey, and we had far more than we could use. It just happened that way. The extractor was too big to handle alone, and I

needed Jill's help. Aren't wives supposed to be helpmates—
or helpers—to their husbands? And selling the honey became her responsibility, because she was home during the
day and had a sanguine personality, which made her a natural salesperson. The problem was that we had so many cases
of honey that she decided, without telling me, that she
would cut the price and sell it quickly. When I heard that
she was selling the honey for three dollars a quart, I couldn't
believe it. I told her that as long as she would work the
bees and get stung, it was OK for her to sell the honey for
three dollars a quart, but that if I was the one getting stung,
the honey was worth far more. That didn't go over very
well.

(Jill) Now let's get back to the chickens. The ones that
survived that terrible storm grew up. Two of them became
the meanest roosters this side of the Rockies. They would
turn on us and attack with their spurs. Jeremy would try to
defend himself, but Jonathan would scream in terror when
either one would come close.

One day when Allan was home, one of the roosters began his fancy footwork, getting ready to attack. Allan picked
up the closest thing handy—a length of 2 by 4 lumber—
and threw it at the rooster to keep him from attacking the
boys and to teach the rooster a lesson. The rooster fell
over with a broken leg, and the boys immediately began
crying for the poor, hurt bird. So Allan, feeling bad, grabbed
an old towel, wrapped up the rooster, and before I knew it,
I heard the door open to two crying boys, a harassed husband, and a moaning, almost lifeless rooster. They laid him
on the kitchen table and instead of wringing his neck and

cooking the old bird for chicken noodle soup, they carefully took tongue depressors and splinted his leg. Greatly humbled, he hobbled around for the next couple of weeks, and eventually we sold him for the neighbor's chicken soup!

The hens laid a constant supply of eggs, and by the time Jeremy was four years old, it became his job to sell them. Jeremy would pull his little red wagon up the path to the chicken house, where he would fill the watering containers and gather the eggs in a little bucket, with me watching from the kitchen window. Every week, he sold several dozen eggs to the employees at the hospital where Allan worked. Eventually, both boys became involved in the egg business, and each had a little jar where they saved their money.

By the time Jeremy was ready to start school, we decided to cut back on the egg business and get rid of all but a few hens. Allan had other projects going at the time, and we were trying to watch our cholesterol levels, so we didn't need many eggs for our own use. We advertised the chickens on the local "swap and shop" radio program, and immediately we had callers wanting them. The boys were so excited that the chickens would have a new home. These nice people were going to take them. As we bagged the chickens up in gunny sacks, Jeremy asked the people where the chickens were going to live, and they told him they were buying them for fryers. Since we were vegetarians, Jeremy had no idea what that meant and came over to ask, "Mommy, what does *fryer* mean?" When I explained that they would be eating the chickens, the boys were shocked. A quick huddle between the two, and the boys decided that they wouldn't sell them after all. But I said that it was too late—they had made a business deal and had to go through with it. They pled and begged, but I remained firm, and with solemn sorrow they watched the chickens they were once so eager to get rid of now being carried off to their deaths!

That wasn't the end of our chicken problems, however. About this time a big friendly black snake took up residence near the chicken house, because he loved the eggs. After being frightened several times by reaching under a chicken for eggs, only to feel the cold, clammy, scaled reptile instead of a nice, warm, smooth egg, the boys refused to gather any more eggs. So I went out to help them. I remember the first time my hand touched that snake. I ran out of the chicken house screaming, "Allan, Allan—*you* get the eggs!" He said, "Ah, black snakes won't hurt you. They're good snakes and eat the poisonous ones." But to me, a snake was a snake, and it had to go.

As I returned from taking care of the nursery at the Baptist Church one Sunday evening, Allan and the boys were standing by the chicken house. Allan called to me, "Jill, come help us." He had the friendly black snake, holding its neck between two sticks, with its six-foot body jerking back and forth. The boys had refused to hold the feed sack for Allan to drop the snake into, so that became my job. I held the feed sack open and tried to move it into position. I turned my head so I wouldn't have to look at that ugly, wiggling snake, and then Allan yelled at me for not holding the bag still. I couldn't believe I was rescuing Allan again. Moments later, I felt the weight of the snake in the sack and knew our project had been successful.

Rescuing Allan

Allan dumped the snake down by the road a mile or so away, by an abandoned house, hoping it would stay and eat mice. But apparently the snake liked eggs better than mice, and a few days later it was back. Once more the snake was bagged, and this time I gave explicit directions to Allan to take it across the state line. He didn't go that far, but it was far enough that we never saw the snake again.

When we got out of the chicken business, Allan decided his boys were budding entrepreneurs who now needed another project, and as he said, "Every boy needs a dog." So the idea took hold that we should raise Australian Shepherds.

I didn't want Australian Shepherds, let alone puppies. I had loved our first dog, Bruno, a Saint Bernard, and when he died, I would have liked to have had another. But Allan thought Australian Shepherds were more practical, so we became the proud owners of Heidi and Snow, two females with blue eyes. Then he suggested that the boys should invest their savings in a male Australian Shepherd so they could breed our females and raise puppies.

Allan wanted to teach the boys early the value of money and the pride of ownership, so he had them take their piggy banks with all their coins to a nearby county, where the meterman had a friend who raised Australian Shepherds and had a large black tricolor male we named Callahan. Years later, the meterman saw Callahan and asked, "Is this the same dog the boys had to count out their money on the pavement and pay for?"

What followed after that were years of breeding puppies. I always told Allan if we were going to raise dogs, we should have a kennel and do it properly. But alas, we never had a kennel, so Heidi would run off into the woods and hide her puppies, and we'd have to go look for them, carry them home, and put them in the doghouse. She, of course, would take them back and hide them again, until we won and Heidi gave up and finally left them in the doghouse.

Heidi finally died, and it was only a few months until Christmas when Allan brought home Princess, a red merle Australian Shepherd.

I'm not an animal person, so those dogs were never allowed in my house. One night we came home to find all three dogs sleeping on the couch! Apparently the door lock hadn't latched when we left, and the wind had blown it open, so the dogs took advantage of this opportunity to live in luxury!

I am allergic to fleas, don't like Australian Shepherds, hated the hassle of puppies, and got angry every time I accidently stepped in their poop. There was no railing on our porch and as soon as the puppies discovered how to climb up on the porch, they would poop there and sometimes fall off. All this would have been avoided if we'd had a kennel.

One day as I was taking a puppy to sell it, it vomited all over the place. I had to put Jeremy in the back of the truck because there wasn't enough room in the cab for all of us and the vomit. We had to stop at a friend's house before we got into town to clean up the mess. The boys were late for school, I couldn't find the lady who wanted to buy the dog, and had to keep it with me at the school until she finally arrived. Once again I ended up doing things I really didn't want to do, all because of Allan.

The interesting thing is that Allan's projects, which were intended to make money, were mostly break-even projects that didn't begin to pay for the stress, worry, and hours of attention that I had to give them. As I write, a new litter has just been born and, thank goodness, Jeremy now has a driver's license and can take the dogs to the vet, get their tails cropped, and feed and worm them. Unfortunately, they still poop on the porch, and I accidently step in it occasionally and have to suffer the embarrassment of this unfavorable aroma that lingers on my shoes as I go to various appointments!

Next, Allan got the great idea that he wanted to build his own sawmill. There was a fellow who came and lived in his van on our property for a short time to help Allan with this project. We also had a couple with two little kids living in a bus who had come from Florida to help. I had no idea why Allan needed a sawmill, but I figured it was just one more of his dreams that he wanted to fulfill, and I knew that once he got it in his head to do something, it was useless to try and change his mind, so I went along. He had it built in our driveway, since that was the only level place close to the house. After the mill was completed came the work of felling the timber, dragging it to the mill, and stacking it. Then we ended up with a huge pile of sawdust right by our back door.

The people involved soon moved on, and since Allan didn't have time to run it, he decided we should try to sell the sawmill. I advertised it in the paper, put it on the "Swap and Shop" radio program, and after showing it several times, an old man responded who had plenty of money and wanted a toy, so he bought it. He gave us, as a part of the sale, a free ticket to raft down the Hiwassee. By the time we wanted to go down the Hiwassee, which was seven years later, I couldn't find the ticket. But the man remembered us, and we got our free ride!

As I recall, rather than making money, we broke even once again. But the boys had a grand time in the sawdust pile, and I guess when I count up the many contented hours they spent playing with their trucks in that, it was worth it.

As a boy, Allan had read a story about a family who had paid for their farm by selling Christmas trees that were growing on their place. I guess Allan is a romantic, because while the boys were little, he leased land, we planted ten thousand white pines, and the dream started to become reality. No one could realize what a job it was to trim the roots, plant, and then mow around ten thousand trees. Our fingers nearly froze trying to plant the seedlings in the cold, snowy March soil. And every time we had to mow around those trees, we realized once again the immensity of the project. Over the next twelve years, we dealt with many Christmas tree challenges. Mowing, shearing, cutting, selling, and baling trees. Moving equipment and coordinating hired help—all of this took time. I was resentful at first, but we were working together as a family, so that helped. Also, having the extra income at Christmas time put all the hard work on the trees in a brighter perspective. But if you really factored in all the time we spent on those Christmas trees, I really wonder if it was worth it. Allan kept reminding me of the substantial tax write-off this project brought to our family. The way I finally made this project worthwhile to me was to spend a little extra money and turn the Christmas tree business into a mission project by giving a free religious book to each person who bought a tree!

(Allan) There were other benefits that came from that Christmas tree project. Before the farm was sold and the trees had grown bigger than most homes needed, it was time to call it quits and reward the boys for all their hard work. Knowing that the boys desperately wanted a four-wheeler, I called the Yamaha dealer and arranged to buy a YZ-80 dirt bike. On the ruse of helping friends move some things, the boys and Jill stopped "just to look" at the Yamahas. Not seeing anything with a Kennedy tag, Jill pulled out the check and asked if they might have something for the Kennedys in exchange for a check. The boys were elated, to say the least, and I'm proud to say they have become willing and skilled workers. I only wish I could have been there to see their faces at the time.

(Jill) Somewhere in the maze of years came the pumpkins. Allan had seen pumpkins that had painted pictures on them that were selling well in the markets. Allan by this time thought I could do anything, and since I had taken a few art classes, certainly I could at least paint pumpkins. So we took the ferry across the Tennessee River to Dayton to a big pumpkin farm, and the boys had a wonderful time searching through a couple of acres of pumpkins for just the right ones to paint. We ended up purchasing a pickup truck load. By the time we got home, Allan was beginning to think more rationally and realized I really didn't have time to paint those pumpkins, so we called a friend in our church who does artwork. She thought it would be a nice idea, but she, too, became too busy to paint them, so they ended up being stored in her cool garage for a couple of months.

By the time we thought about the pumpkins again, it was after Halloween and getting close to Thanksgiving. So one day when Jonathan and I were in town with the truck, we decided to go pick up the pumpkins. Now, what should we do with them? The last thing I was about to do was to paint the things. I figured that since Allan was not around, it would be much more fun to give them away than to try and sell them. So on the four-mile stretch between town and home, we stopped at all the neighbors and gave away these specially selected, perfect-sized pumpkins to be cut up and used for Thanksgiving pies. One little girl about five years old, living close to poverty, asked in surprise, "Is this pumpkin for me? Wow! Now my granny can make me a real pumpkin pie!" Just to see how every person's face lighted up with surprise when given something they didn't expect really made my day. Of all the projects in which I helped rescue Allan, I think this ended the best!

But Allan's projects didn't end with the pumpkins. He tried raising squash and pumpkins, rebuilding and selling wrecked cars, cutting Black Locust posts and poles, and cutting and selling firewood. One thing can be said about Allan—he isn't lazy. It just seems that his projects always grow beyond the time and effort he is able to give them, and he needs me to tie up the loose ends.

Why have I resented Allan's projects?

First, I resented having to work our lives away, when I didn't think we needed the money. I didn't want my boys growing up thinking making money should be their primary objective in life, as it appeared to be with Allan.

I was content with living a simple life. If I had just enough extra money to entertain friends with and enough money for gas so I could do church visitation and run errands for people, I could be happy. The other things money can buy were nice but not really necessary for me to be happy.

Second, these projects robbed us of time spent doing fun things together with Allan. I didn't want Jeremy and Jonathan thinking that making money was more important than family and relationships.

But the third and real reason for my resentment is that I felt controlled by these projects. My participation was expected—and no matter how much I did, I never felt my efforts were really appreciated.

Allan and I were caught in a compliant/aggressive-controller conflict. I was the compliant one who felt intimidated and inferior to Allan. After all, he had a graduate degree, a high-status professional career, and seemed to know it all. I didn't have a college degree or a money-making job outside the home, and I certainly didn't know all the things Allan knew. Allan became the aggressive-controller who used my time and talents. It wasn't as if he didn't ask for my opinion. Allan says he asked, and I'm sure he did—but because I didn't think I could say No and still be loved, I didn't really believe I had the luxury of saying No to him. The irony of it all is that while I was feeling controlled by Allan, he had no idea I felt this way.

All he knew was that much of the time I ignored his "things to do" list for his projects, so he interpreted my actions as being irresponsible. This made him even more critical of me, and I reacted by nagging him to be more involved. We were really in a vicious, dysfunctional cycle.

I learned that the way to break this cycle was for me to risk communicating with Allan about my feelings. He didn't want to be controlling. Allan felt his mother was controlling, and he knew how that affected him. But because I was unwilling to let him know how I was feeling, he fell into the same pattern of behavior he had seen modeled in his home.

I'm learning to set limits and to make them as specific as possible so that Allan knows my boundaries and I don't need to feel resentful of him. This has been hard for me, because even while growing up I hated conflict and gave up my own desires rather than risk a confrontation. I never learned that it was OK to stick up for what I wanted. Being liked was so important to me that I tended to be a pushover, if that meant having friends. Even at home, where I felt displaced from my favorite-child status when my brother John was born, I tried hard to please, thinking that was what it took to be loved.

While I'm learning to set limits, Allan is learning to respect my limits and not to use the power of his superior knowledge, skills, or quick insight to cower me into submissiveness.

The more I feel his genuine, unconditional love for me, the easier it is for me to reveal my true feelings. What a sense of freedom unconditional love gives!

Now, when Allan suggests something, I seldom think, "Oh, here we go again." I enjoy adventure, and as long as it is new and fun and we can work together on it, I don't mind participating. What makes it fun is knowing I have the choice—and knowing that regardless of my choice, I'll still be loved.

After twenty-two years of rescuing Allan in his various projects, I read an interesting statement from a book by Dr. Henry Cloud and Dr. John Townsend entitled *Boundaries*. "Women who fail to set boundaries and say yes to things that are forced upon them, sometimes say no to sex in marriage as the one area in an unhealthy relationship where they can have control." I wondered, were the authors talking about me?

CHAPTER

9

Sex Isn't a Four-Letter Word

(**Allan**) When Jill and I got married, I looked forward to the honeymoon—as all healthy males do. I had visions of how great our sex life would be. My education in the art of sexual love, however, was nonexistent. My folks never talked of such things, and I can't remember them touching or kissing, besides just a peck, in the presence of us kids. No one pulled me aside before the wedding and said, "Allan, let me give you a few tips." We didn't even have premarital counseling.

Just about all I knew about sex came from the few pictures I'd once seen in a *Playboy* magazine and the descriptions of sexual escapades from the James Bond books I had read. But I figured I knew enough that without question, ecstasy was right around the corner. After all, Jill, with her flirtatious ways, was sure to be the most exciting sexual partner a man could have.

But I soon learned that having the right equipment wasn't the answer if you didn't know how to use it. And Jill and I didn't. I knew nothing about the needs of a woman. I just knew about the expectations of a man—and that was to have sex and to have it frequently. I didn't know how to woo, caress, and wait. I had no idea that sex started in the kitchen at breakfast, grew with little attentions throughout the day, blossomed with compliments and nonsexual touching in the evening, and culminated with tenderness, compassion, and long uninterrupted time to hold and to touch.

For me, sex was an event. Years later I learned that for Jill, sex was an environment. Unfortunately, I did little during the first decade of marriage to create a responsive environment for Jill. I'd leave early in the morning, often before she was awake. Or if she was up, I'd tell her all the things on my agenda she needed to do, then I'd head out the door until late in the evening. If I called during the day, it was to get an update and give her more instructions, not to tell her how much she meant to me and how much I loved her. When I did get home, all I would notice was the messy house, nothing on the table, and all the things on my list she hadn't done—or hadn't done the way I thought they should be done. After the children came, she was always with the boys. Instead of appreciating her as a good mother, many times I was jealous and resentful, especially when she used them as an excuse not to come to bed with me.

I didn't realize how one's childhood can skew one's attitude toward sex. Jill and I had never talked about sex during our courtship. I had no idea that she had picked up the notion that sex was a four-letter word. She'd heard enough gossip about certain relatives making out, shacking up, and playing around that she had come to believe that sex was a dirty thing—and certainly not a part of the life of a good Christian girl—single or married. The consequences of the sexual escapades of others had led Jill to determine that she would never be a part of such vulgarity. Sex was for having babies—not for pleasure. It didn't help that before our wedding the few comments Jill did hear about sex in marriage didn't put men in a very favorable light.

Instead of viewing the area of sexuality as risque or taboo, I wish that before marriage we could have been open enough to discuss questions such as, "What are your attitudes about sex? Your expectations? What did your parents tell you about sex? What about your friends? Why do you think God created sex? How do you think sex can contribute to a healthy marriage? Is there ever a time when a married couple shouldn't have sex? Are there certain things a married couple shouldn't do when having sex? How do you think a man's sexual needs differ from a woman's? When you think about experiencing sex with me for the first time on our honeymoon, how do you feel? How often do you think a married couple should come together sexually? What do you think you'll enjoy most about the sexual experience? Is there anything you feel you wouldn't like? Did you have any past experiences that may have shaped your attitude about sex?"

If we would have asked those questions and discussed this whole area of sexuality, perhaps we could have discovered the red flags and would have realized we needed to begin our lives together with understanding and a deeper appreciation of our different individual expectations and needs.

I thought prudishness died with Queen Victoria, so I was shocked to discover that I had married a woman with Victorian attitudes about sex. And frankly, I didn't know what to do about it. Do you go up to your dad and say, "Jill won't have sex with me"? Do you go up to your pastor and say, "What do you do to get your wife to have sex?" Of course not—he'd think I was weird. Men are supposed to know these things. After all, Jill and I were active in the leadership of the church and looked like the perfect, happily married couple. So I suffered in silence.

During the first eight or so years of our married lives, "No" was where I felt we lived sexually. "No" wasn't the exception—it was the rule! I remember wondering just what it would take to move the answer to "Yes." My reactions to her rejection of my sexual advances were many and varied. They ranged from demanding my rights to withdrawing into my shell and feeling unloved and unappreciated to feelings of defiance and thinking, "Well, if that's the way you feel, my needs can be met somewhere else!" I'm embarrassed to say that sometimes I looked at other women and wondered what they would be like in bed. A couple of times, I went against everything I had been taught growing up and yielded to the temptation of buying a *Playboy* to enjoy the feelings I'd get feasting on those pictures. Usually though, I merely lost myself in forging a homestead out of our land and expended my excess energy by long hours on the job.

The longer things went on this way, the more I found myself focusing on what I wanted and needed. Out of frustration, I became busier and busier. I looked for other things to meet my needs of belonging, love, and self-worth. As I focused more on myself, any needs Jill might have had became secondary. I would think, "I'm not getting what I expected out of this relationship. Something is going to have to change." I didn't understand the dynamics of a healthy give-and-take marriage relationship.

(Jill) I had no idea how important it was for a wife to meet her husband's sexual needs. I didn't even realize a Christian man should have any, beyond wanting to have children. Nor did I realize I had sexual needs—or how a woman's body will respond to stimulation. I can't believe I was so naive.

It wasn't as if I didn't have an opportunity to learn. Before marriage, Mom Kennedy gave me a book, and during the early years, Allan's Aunt P.K. gave me some audio tapes. But frankly, I had such a warped attitude about sex that a book or tape weren't enough to turn me around. I scarcely glanced at the book and don't even remember listening to the tapes.

I had seen some relatives who were so hung up on sex that it had become an addiction. I didn't want that to happen to me, so I figured the less I'd do it, the better. And to avoid addiction, I tried hard not to enjoy it, for fear I would want more and end up like so many of my relatives, living merely for self-gratification. When Allan brought home a book entitled, *God Invented Sex*, I was mortified. I couldn't believe anyone would be so brash as to put "God" and "sex" in the same title.

I had no model of a healthy sexual life from my folks. Now that I think back, I can remember a rare attempted kiss by one that was rejected by the other. But I don't remember the spontaneous hugs and kisses, the tender touches and endearing words, that I now know are a part of a healthy marriage.

I entered marriage wanting to be a good wife. I tried hard to meet Allan's needs, but because of the way I was treated, I had little desire to meet his sexual and emotional needs. I avoided snuggling for fear it would lead to something more, and I generally avoided Allan during the evening hours, busying myself with the boys. Many nights I wouldn't even go to bed until I was sure Allan had fallen asleep.

Because I could see the tendency in Allan to do things to an excess, such as overworking, I was afraid that if I gave in to Allan's sexual desires too often, he'd only want more, and I would possibly be contributing to what I feared might become an addiction. I loved Allan, but he was so critical of what I said that I felt that if I expressed my feelings or asked questions about our sexual relationship, I would be misunderstood and criticized. So I never said anything. Besides, I thought I knew what was best for him. Obviously, I was wrong. Dead wrong. And my attitude almost destroyed the very thing I was trying to protect.

To be truthful, I didn't enjoy sex during those early years.

There was no tender, loving care. I felt used. It seemed that Allan was doing it for his own pleasure. And in my book, self-gratification was a sin. I did it only because I knew it was a wifely duty.

I was shocked into change, however, out of fear of losing Allan. If I had to pinpoint a day when this all came to a head, it was the day we were heading to North Carolina for a family reunion. Jeremy was two and a half, and I was pregnant with Jonathan. Allan was working hard to make this outing fun for the family. On our way, we stopped to let Jeremy play in the river. I sat on a rock dipping my feet in the cool water—and at that moment, the water was as cold as our relationship. We had both recently expressed that we had no feelings for each other. We were empty. There was just nothing there. Attempting to be civil and to make conversation, I asked about the woman's face on the T-shirt Allan was wearing. He acknowledged it was someone he had met at a hospital meeting and that she had sent it to his office as a gift, thinking he wasn't married. (Emotionally, we weren't!) When I heard about that shirt, I was devastated. I was angry and confused and realized I had more feelings for Allan than I had thought. I didn't want this relationship to slip away. But what could I do?

This crisis drove me to reach out for help, and I spoke to our pastor's wife. She had grown to be a good and trustworthy friend with whom I could be vulnerable. She helped me to begin to see things differently.

I sensed I was not meeting Allan's sexual needs and that he might be driven to look elsewhere. So I determined to say "Yes" to sex even though I wouldn't at first let myself enjoy it—because my mind still put sex in the gutter. It's hard to let go of those old scripts. It takes education, decided effort, and the Holy Spirit's nudging to bury the old and begin to write healthy new scripts. Change gradually took place. I'm often reminded of the text in John 13:17: "If you know these things, happy are you if you do them"(NKJV). This became the formula that gradually brought about a change in attitude. I knew it was right to pleasure my husband sexually. I did it, and the feelings of pleasure followed for me. For too long I had allowed my feelings to dictate my actions.

After I made this decided effort to do what I knew was right and kept telling myself that it was OK to enjoy our sexual relationship, I overheard two older women who were good Christians. They were talking about the large Jacuzzi whirlpool bath in the house one of them had just built, and suddenly I heard the other exclaim, "Isn't sex fun!" I couldn't believe my ears. But that comment got me to thinking. They weren't newlyweds! They were at least fifteen or twenty years older than I was, and they thought sex was fun? Maybe it got better with time. I was determined to find out!

Now, I've discovered, they were right! If only I had known all this before marriage. If only I had had a healthy sexual model to follow from my own family. I determined my boys wouldn't be sexually handicapped as both Allan and I had been.

(Allan) I agree with Jill. I want our boys to have a healthy attitude toward sex, and all the wholesome, accurate infor-

7—L.B.L.

mation they can get before marriage. I don't want them to suffer the frustration and agony we went through. But more than this, I want them to see that sex is something beautiful that God created to bring fulfillment to both husband and wife. I want them to see love modeled in our home and mutual respect for each other through nonsexual touching and little acts of kindness. I also want them to understand how easily the sexual beauty in marriage can be compromised with such things as entertaining thoughts of other women or looking at pornographic pictures. I want them to have enough information to make better choices than I did.

Jill and I are still learning about each other and how to better meet each other's sexual needs, but that's what marriage is all about. That's why it never gets old, just better!

10

Changing Points

(Allan) Change, for most, is like the ripening of an apple. The process is slow. First there's the blush of pink on the sunny side. The apple is still green, but it's in the process of becoming what God envisioned it to become: red, ripe, and juicy. If you stand and watch, you won't notice the change. But time-lapse photography can catch it. Or if you busy yourself with other things and check again after a week or so, you'll notice the difference. It may appear to you, the casual observer, as if an abrupt change from green to red has taken place, but in reality, it happened little by little.

That's the way change happens in marriage. There may be change points that trigger the ripening process, but change seldom happens overnight. It's a process of learning—of trial and error. Old destructive behaviors don't magically disappear. But when love becomes a decision on the part of one, or hopefully both, the frequency of their occurrence is diminished. But it's not until the destructive habits are replaced with positive behaviors that change becomes evident. So it was in the ripening process that Jill and I experienced in our marriage.

For Jill, it was in her seventh month of pregnancy, sitting there by the Pigeon River, splashing her toes in the icy water, watching Jeremy play, and suddenly looking up and focusing on the woman's face on my T-shirt. I hadn't really worn it to provoke a reaction in Jill. The face of the woman on the shirt meant little to me. It was merely a clean shirt that I happened to pull out of my drawer and put on.

I could tell, though, after Jill mentioned the shirt, that it was a knife in her heart. My feelings for Jill, however, had cooled to such a low that I didn't really care. I didn't mean to hurt her, but I didn't feel sorry for hurting her either. I suppose unconsciously I was feeling that she deserved to feel hurt for the many times she had hurt me by not meeting my needs.

But for Jill, that was a change point.

My first blush of pink centered on the birth of Jonathan. There was no question that this birth would have to be a Cesarean section, as had been the last. So we had the luxury of choosing the date rather than having nature impose it upon us. Since I was in administration at the hospital, I had the privilege of going into surgery to watch. Our pastor's wife, Richa, a special friend of ours and a nurse, gowned with me, and we were positioned in a corner so as not to be in the way. I remember the anesthetist saying, "OK," and the surgeons starting the incision. I instinctively moved forward for a better look. What I saw turned out to be the most shaking experience of my life. In just thirty-seven seconds, Jonathan was out and handed to the pediatrician—and by the time I asked what they were doing, they were closing!

As I saw Jill's abdomen cut open and bleeding, something happened in my heart. Feelings of love I had thought were long buried came rushing to the surface. Jill, my Jill, had suffered like this to have a baby she knew we wanted so badly. Having gone through the first Cesarean birth and knowing the second would be the same, I was overcome with her commitment to me to be willing to go through it all again. It had to be love.

I responded with feelings of love, humility, and awe, mixed with sorrow and remorse over the way I had treated her at times. I determined that things were going to change. I wanted to be a loving and kind husband and father, but I didn't know how to change things at home in a constructive way. My childhood home had been neat and orderly, with good meals on a regular schedule. I knew that my stress level was a lot less when the house was in order and there were regular mealtimes. It gave me a sense of inner peace. But life at our home seemed more like controlled confusion. Somehow, in trying to relate to Jill's lack of organization, I had become critical and overbearing.

Just knowing that the feelings of love were still there between us gave me the psychological energy to try again. Unfortunately, energy without knowledge is not necessarily productive. We didn't yet have the tools that it took to be what we wanted to be.

I've discovered marriage to be something like a team of horses in a harness. It works best when they pull together. Marriage can move forward, just as a wagon does, when one of the team decides to forge ahead without the other. It takes greater effort on the part of one, and energy is soon spent, but progress can be made. Then it might be that the other catches the vision and plods ahead, and the roles are reversed. And that's just about where Jill and I were. We were in the harness—we were committed—but we weren't yet pulling together. If anything, Jill may have been in the lead. Even though I hadn't let her know, I had noticed that she was trying hard to make our marriage work.

Two years later, after Jill weaned Jonathan, she began urging me to go to a Marriage Encounter weekend, thinking it would help us. Each time a weekend was scheduled in our area, however, I came up with good reasons why it was impossible for me to go. Then it happened; I ran out of excuses. With no conflicting appointments, I reluctantly agreed to attend.

Once there, I realized that the things being said by the presenters were speaking to my felt needs. They were offering me relational tools I wished I could have had ten years ago when we got married. I began to see a glimmer of hope that with these communication skills, we could get our marriage together. I really got into the program. I got to know myself better by getting in touch with some of my feelings and learned what motivated me to do and say some of the things I did. I was eager to follow the presenters' instructions to write out how we felt about certain issues and then to dialogue with Jill. As I shared my feelings with her in that secure, love-based environment, it was as if a load of guilt fell away. I felt much like John Bunyan's Pilgrim did when his heavy pack rolled off his back. I was free—free to love and live again.

But just as I began to pull ahead, Jill lagged behind. She didn't want to write and resisted discussing the various issues with me. Would I as a man ever be able to understand the mind of a woman?

(Jill) I went to that weekend knowing that Allan was the problem. If he would just be understanding and kind, bring me flowers occasionally and not try to change me, everything would be OK. But as I listened to the presentations, I was shocked with the revelation that I might be the source of many of our problems. I was confused, feeling guilty, and vulnerable. I was still afraid of Allan's criticism. If I were to write what they asked and reveal my feelings of guilt and sorrow, it would just open Pandora's box. It was a crack in my armor that I didn't want Allan to see for fear he would take advantage of the situation to strike another blow. The risk was too great. So I simply refused to write.

It was not until the second afternoon, twenty or more hours after the weekend had begun, that my defenses started to crumble. Allan was writing his feelings and sharing them with me. He was risking vulnerability. In love, couldn't I do the same? It wasn't an intellectual decision I made to begin writing and sharing but was in direct response to the love I felt from him. He was filling me for the first time in a long time. How could I not in love respond? I repeated over and over again the words on the banner in the presentation room, "Love is a decision . . . Love is a decision." My love decision was to open my armor wide to Allan by sharing my feelings, and in the process we began to experience the intimacy we were craving. It was an incredible high for both of us.

(Allan) I began to see what an impact the things I did and said had on Jill's life. The disrespectful way I had been treating her was literally destroying whatever positive feelings she once had about herself and me. And this then affected the way she viewed me and the rest of the world. We started learning how to share on a feeling level instead of on a factual level. This was new for us. Jill was afraid to express her true feelings, and like so many other men, I had been taught to push feelings out of the way and not confuse them with facts. Now I began to see that feelings merely *were*. They weren't good or bad. But they were powerful. They were the key to one's actions. We may have been sleeping in the same bed, parenting the same two boys, and living in the same house, but we were poles apart when it came to our relationship with each other.

Each of us were the product of our parents' gene pool, plus the experiences we had passed through in life. Heredity and environment had shaped us differently, including the way we had been taught to communicate. I began to see that there were a number of listening habits—or more specifically, nonlistening habits—which I had acquired that interfered with my ability to receive communication. Sometimes I found myself listening simply to identify points for argument or rebuttal. Or when talking or negotiating with others, I tended to hear what I wanted to hear. Both Jill and I experienced the fear of change. If we stopped to listen to each other, we might learn that we needed to change in some way. Since change is hard, many times we'd feel like shouting, "Don't tell me. I don't want to know. I might have to do something I don't want to do."

That weekend, it became apparent that one of the barriers to my understanding Jill was that I wouldn't stop long enough to hear her out without interrupting to offer solutions or try to fix things. I needed to *listen* to what she had to say. I had a tendency to interrupt her over the validity of some minor detail and never wait to hear her side of the story. Other problems I noticed were that I would impatiently announce a solution, not waiting for Jill to talk about the situation as she saw it. This was especially shortsighted of me, since this tendency made her increasingly anticipate that I would announce a solution before she had time for problem analysis and resolution.

The answer to these and other listening problems was to concentrate totally on listening to Jill. When I was in school, I would concentrate on what my professors were saying and take notes. I began to wonder what would happen if I gave Jill that same kind of attention when she was talking to me.

(Jill) I can't let Allan take all the blame for our communication problems. Many times in the past, I hadn't given Allan my full attention, especially when he began telling me what to do and how to do it. I appeared to be listening, but I wasn't, because I felt inferior and sorry for myself. I also told myself that it was what Allan said to me and how he acted that made me feel inferior and depressed.

On our Marriage Encounter weekend, I learned that I create my feelings by what I tell myself about what is being said to me or happening to me. When I accepted Allan's criticism and blame, I promptly told myself that I was incompetent and worthless, without any evaluation on my part. Feeling incompetent and worthless was snuffing out one of my important needs—that of self-worth—and I blamed Allan.

When Allan interpreted my frequent "No" to his sexual advances as rejection of him, he felt rejected and depressed. The reality was that I was reacting from a distorted view of sexual love. The truth that helped to free us to grow and understand each other began with accepting responsibility for our own emotional feelings.

Our communication leapt forward when we could talk without blaming the other person. Now we could express and listen to negative feelings such as anger, discouragement, or disappointment and not feel guilt for having produced these feelings in the other person.

Because our love for each other was growing, we tried not to do or say those things that might be interpreted as a lack of love or caring for one another. Understanding that Allan and I are not responsible *for* one another in any way but that we are responsible *to* one another in every way was just one more step in helping us develop good communication skills.

Allan is quick-thinking—it takes me longer to process information. Allan can express himself well in words—I don't always. It takes me time to formulate answers and make plans. That's why I was so glad the presenters stressed listening with your whole heart and being, with every fiber stretched to the full, letting your spouse know that you care about them and what they have to say.

I learned that I could encourage Allan to tell me more by saying, "I think I understand," "Tell me more about that," or "That's interesting." Questions were OK if I needed more information to get a handle on what was going on inside Allan, but I had to watch it so that it didn't sound as if I had put him on the witness stand and was interrogating him. Too many "Why" questions make a person feel defensive. But questions that start with "Is this the way you . . ." or "Do you . . ." can get me the information I need without sounding so judgmental.

It's so easy for me to jump to conclusions or demand my own way. I learned that I could keep out of a lot of hot water if I'd just be more observant to the hidden meaning behind Allan's words or listen to what he was trying to tell me with his body language.

I'll never forget the time Allan was standing in the church foyer shaking hands as people were leaving. As I passed him to go outside, where I loved to stand around and visit with people, I realized the weather had turned cold. Since I'm always colder than Allan, he would often let me wear his suit coat. So as I passed, I said to him, "I'm cold, give me your coat."

Allan hesitated, and his reply startled me, "No, you can't have my coat."

I retorted, "I'm your wife, I'm cold, and I want your coat." He looked around at the crush of people and meekly removed his coat. A few minutes later, I noticed that instead of standing where he could shake hands with people, he was standing with his back in the corner at the end of the coat rack away from the crowd. I finally went up to him and asked, "What are you doing over here?"

He then explained that when he had been on the platform getting up from kneeling following the prayer, he had ripped out the seat of his suit pants. Because I wasn't willing to listen to his body language and he wasn't wanting to start a holy war in the church foyer and risk the embarrassment of a public explanation about why he wouldn't give me his coat, he merely surrendered his coat to me and put his backside into a corner! Needless to say, I felt terrible about what I had done, and he promptly got his coat back. But all this could have been avoided if I had merely listened to more than what Allan's words were telling me.

(Allan) The first time I really listened to Jill on that Marriage Encounter weekend was when we wrote to each other about a time of special closeness in our lives and then dialogued about it. Jill wrote about the time my mom died. We all knew it was coming—she had been fighting cancer for three years. Jill and Mom were good friends. During our engagement, she helped Jill plan our wedding and reception and learn homemaking skills. After we were married, Jill became her third daughter, and they spent many hours together as mothers and daughters do, shopping, sewing, cooking and canning, and sharing spiritual concerns and insights. Mom was always there when Jill needed her. Jill was like a sponge, soaking up Mom's accumulated years of wisdom and skills. But in spite of this, I had no idea about the void Mom's death had left in Jill's life, and how in death Mom had contributed to our closeness, until I read what Jill had written:

> Dearest Allan, my prayer is that through closeness and unity with Christ, we will have closeness and unity in our relationship—not for the moment, but daily and then eternally. As I reflect on times of closeness and unity in our marriage, I sense the closest time was at the death of our mom. There was an enormous void, and we both saw shades of gray in the emptiness that surrounded us. There were silent times, sharing times, and tearful times as we made the three-and-a-half-hour drive home for the memorial service. I remember how together, we told our boys, who were one and three years old at the time, "We know that someday we will see our mom, because she was so close to God." I want you and me and our sons to determine in our hearts to have that kind of experience. I turned to you at that time, and you helped mend the hurt. God took something bitter and made it sweet through our relationship.

This sharing helped me realize just how much Jill had lost when Mom died. My family had been a family of many strengths, and Jill had relied heavily on my mom for counsel and encouragement. When Mom died, Jill lost more than a friend and needed me to help fill the void. I hadn't realized it before, but now, by listening to Jill's hurt, I was drawn to her like a magnet. The real lesson we learned, as we shared the memories of that moment of closeness, was that as wonderful as human friends and family are, there is no friend like God. He's our true source of strength. This experience made me realize for the first time that the sharing of deep inner feelings was perhaps the strongest bonding agent in the world. I loved the sense of intimacy it brought to Jill and me, and I mourned more than the death of my mom. I mourned the lost years of intimacy with Jill because previously we had communicated facts rather than feelings. I determined then that there would be no more lost years. Jill was too precious to me.

But resolve is often stronger than reality, and although we got better at sharing feelings, my bad habits of telling instead of listening still seeped to the surface.

A major change point for me came the day my pastor and friend made the simple comment to me, "Allan, you have a precious flower in Jill. Just make sure you don't crush her."

I simmered for months afterward when I thought of that comment. What did he truly know about our relationship? What right did he have in presuming I was crushing Jill? He didn't see the way the house looked during the week when we lived in it. It was clean when he came to visit! We even had good food when he came. I had almost concluded that the only way for me to get good food and a clean house was to invite company over!

I thought I had effectively communicated to Jill my desire for a clean, neat house and regular tasty meals—even to the point that I would ask if she understood what my expectations were. When she'd meekly reply Yes, I'd retort, "Well, why aren't those expectations met? Just what don't you understand about them? What's the problem?" The problem, I began to realize, was that my method of communicating so alienated Jill that she was angered to the point of not caring what I wanted and rebelled by choosing not to cooperate. This ongoing issue cast a shadow over everything else in our lives, including sex. Who wants to make love with a bear?

I felt trapped—a prisoner in my own home. The heightened level of communication that Marriage Encounter had brought us had helped, but it hadn't changed the basic problem. For the next couple of years, we seemed to be in a rut, not knowing how to get out or how to go on. We were committed to each other. We were married and were going to stay that way. But where was the passion, the fire, the romance? Yes, there was sex—we had boys to prove it—but it seemed that there was a difference between being married and doing what married people do and being in love.

Over the next several months, I began to realize that if I were to be truly honest with myself, there were many times I didn't want to go home. I didn't like being there much of the time. It was far more enjoyable to do what I liked without the pressure and stress of being somewhere where I experienced confusion and discord. I began to face the truth. I could successfully run a multimillion-dollar business, but I was a failure at home!

Finally, I decided that some changes had to be made. I

came to the realization that more than ten years of trying to change Jill had failed. If changes were to be made, I would have to change the only person I could possibly control—me! I resolved that without telling Jill, I was going to quit telling her what to do, what to think, and how to act. I would keep my administrative role for the office. Instead, I would try to involve her in decisions and work together as a team, even though I might think I knew best. I would listen to her and make sure she was finished before expressing my opinion, if I would give one at all. For eighteen months, I kept reminding myself, "I need to communicate—not tell. Involve Jill. Ask her opinion. Listen. Don't crush the flower God has given you." I had to constantly review my goal to make sure I wouldn't regress to my old habits. And it made an incredible difference in our lives. Finally, one evening, Jill asked me, "What is different about us? Something has changed, but I can't figure out what it is."

Feigning ignorance, I asked what she was talking about. Upon further questioning, I realized she really couldn't pinpoint what it was, but she just knew that something was different about our relationship, and it felt good—very good!

Several months later I confessed to her what I had been trying to do. She simply smiled and said with a sparkle in her eyes, "Well, I knew something was going on!"

That was several years ago now. It has been fun to see the cute smile return, see the twinkle in her eyes come back, and the bounce in her step. At last I had set Jill free to be herself, and in doing so, I got back the Jill I had first grown to love. But now there was an even greater beauty about her—a calmness and joy that comes only when a person feels accepted and loved unconditionally—extravagantly. And in the process, I found the personal peace and contentment I was trying so hard to orchestrate through my overbearing leadership.

One day as I was reading a book about Jesus, I came upon a quotation that pretty much summarizes what I was experiencing with Jill.

"The exercise of force is contrary to the principles of God's government; He desires only the service of love; and love cannot be commanded; it cannot be won by force or authority. Only by love is love awakened."—*The Desire of Ages*, 3.

CHAPTER

11

Growing Spiritually

(Allan) I don't know why I used to think I had arrived when it came to spiritual things. I guess I had my salvation all tied up with belonging to what I thought was the right denomination. Raised in the church, I thought I knew all the answers, but, unfortunately, many times I "talked the talk," as they say, without "walking the walk."

When I first met Jill, I wanted her to go to the same church as I did, not just because I had been taught that the Seventh-day Adventist Church taught Bible truth (even though that was a part of it) but because I loved Jill and I was concerned about her spiritual growth.

I knew, however, that I had to be very careful not to push her into the Adventist church, since I didn't want her to change denominations just because of me. I had seen too many people join a church because they wanted to please a fiancé, only to slip back into their old ways when the newness of marriage wore off.

I shouldn't have worried about Jill's spiritual life, however. Through the years I've seen those qualities of simple, childlike faith I had once thought to be naive, become even more evident in Jill's life, until her faith has burst forth to show itself, I'm embarrassed to admit, to be often far stronger than mine. What Jill may have lacked in religious knowledge, she more than made up for in her growing, daily relationship with Jesus.

After Jill's baptism, I took the role of answering question after question regarding my view of religious doctrine. While being the expert was a heady experience, I soon realized that there was a vast difference between being religious and having a thirst for spiritual things, as Jill had. It became evident to me that an intellectual religion, even if you knew all the Bible answers, was not life-changing, nor did it make one spiritually sensitive. The "good" Christian mask I had developed painstakingly over the years, I found much easier to wear in public than at home. At home it began to crack when Jill brought up the hypocrisy of my ways. It hurt when she said, "I thought you were a Christian. Why don't you act like one?"

I'll admit that there were many times, especially in the early years of our marriage, that I set aside everything I knew about Jesus' commandment to "love one another; as I have loved you" (John 13:34) and ended up treating Jill the way I felt like treating her rather than as Christ would have treated her.

As I have read, studied, and prayed, I have become convinced that mere religion often focuses on the externals—on different versions of the Bible, the latest theological issues, or good books. As important as these may be, they alone don't necessarily help you become more spiritual. Matthew 25:35, 36 makes it plain that those who are welcomed into the kingdom will not be asked, "What books did you read? What doctrines did you believe? What religious debates did you win?" No. Jesus will say, "For I was hungry and you gave Me food; I was thirsty and you gave Me drink; I was a stranger and you took Me in; I was naked and you clothed Me; I was sick and you visited Me; I was in prison and you came to Me" (NKJV).

I may have tutored Jill in Bible knowledge, but she has done far more in tutoring me as to what a spiritual life of unselfish service is really all about. Unfortunately, it has taken me a number of years to realize that instead of focusing on information, what I should have been doing was affirming Jill's daily experience with the Lord as she fulfilled His commission to help others.

(Jill) I think Allan is a little hard on himself. If it weren't for what I saw in Allan's life and the lives of his family members, I doubt I would have been attracted to Adventist Christianity. I grew up steeped in Indian superstitions. I was afraid to walk under a ladder or have a black cat cross my path. In addition, because of my Cherokee ancestry, my mom passed down superstitions she had learned from her mom. I couldn't come in one door and go out another or rock a chair when it was empty or sweep dirt out the door after sundown, or I'd be struck with bad luck! I was even treated with Indian folk remedies. For example, I remember that when I got the croup, we made a trip to the crawdad hole on the other side of town and got some polecat (skunk) grease from Old Sorrow Top, who was the old mother-in-law of a cousin. Old Sorrow Top killed, skinned, gutted, rendered (cooked) it, and drained the grease off the meat. Then she processed it, bottled it, and sold it as a remedy for croup. Well, it just took one spoonful, and I can assure you, I was cured!

So with my background of Indian superstition, window-dressed by what little I did get out of attending Vacation Bible School or Sunday school, I grew up with a Pollyanna-ish view of religion. At eighteen years of age, when I began seriously studying the Bible, I was shocked to learn what it really said about certain issues. For example, what happened when you died? I thought you went straight to heaven, until I found Psalm 146:4—"His breath goeth forth, he returneth to his earth; in that very day his thoughts perish"—and I asked Allan to explain what I was reading. Allan showed me how this text fit with 1 Thessalonians 4:16, 17: "For the Lord himself shall descend from heaven with a shout, with the voice of the archangel, and with the trump of God: and the dead in Christ shall rise first: Then we which are alive and remain shall be caught up together with them in the clouds, to meet the Lord in the air: and so shall we ever be with the Lord." After several days of struggling and weeping with God over this issue, I concluded that sleeping in death until the resurrection at Christ's second coming made a lot of sense. Besides, if you didn't know anything when you were dead, then the moment you were resurrected would be the beginning of that eternal party in heaven that I was looking forward to.

As my Bible knowledge grew, so did my prayer life. I remember in one Bible study group learning about that special group of 144,000 righteous people who are living when Christ returns. (See Revelation 7:4: "And I heard the number of them which were sealed: and there were sealed a hundred and forty and four thousand of all the tribes of the children of Israel.") I thought, *Wow, I'd like to be one of those!* So I started praying and asking, "Lord, how do you get to be part of the 144,000?"

As soon as I prayed that prayer, things started happening in my life that made me realize I had a long way to go to become the person God wanted me to be. I had some things that needed to be cleaned up in my life.

One night I had a vivid dream. I woke with an impression that I should go to a girl I had thrown some rocks at in second grade. A group of kids were picking on her, and I joined the crowd. I'm not happy I did that, but the Lord brought that back to my mind after twenty-five years. "Lord," I prayed, "Are You telling me I should go see Nancy Nichol and that I should tell her I'm sorry?" So I called my mother and asked, "Mother, would you please find Nancy Nichol?" She called around the town where we had lived then and found that Nancy was living about forty miles away in another town. My mother and I went to visit her. Nancy was quite surprised to see me. I shared with her that I was impressed I should come to apologize to her—that I wanted to be ready when the Lord came. She lived in a humble home out in the country. Everything was neat and clean. Her yard was filled with flowers. She told me about her children, and we had a nice visit. Admitting I had sinned wasn't something easy to do, but the sense of release from guilt was exhilarating.

The Lord also brought back to my memory the time that my mother had given me some money for my piano teacher and I kept it instead of giving it to her. So I went to my piano teacher. "Do you remember that when I was in grade school I took piano lessons from you? I didn't pay you for one of those lessons, and I have some money to give you." I gave her the money.

"What's happening in your life?" she asked.

I told her how I had met a young man and that we had married, that I'd found a new religion, and that for the first time in my life it felt wonderful to be doing what God wanted me to do.

"Oh, Seventh-day Adventists?" she asked, "Well, I watch George Vandeman on the *It is Written* television broadcast every Sunday."

I just happened to have some George Vandeman books in the car, so I gave them to her. She was so pleased.

I was also impressed to make it right with Miss Georgia. She had given me green beans from her garden, and a week or so later she asked, "Jill, how were those beans? Did you enjoy them?"

"Oh yes, they were so good," I lied.

Do you know what I actually did with those beans? They molded in my refrigerator, and I fed them to my boys' pony. I couldn't have known if they were good or not. Now I felt I had to apologize to her.

The more I prayed, the more the Lord convicted me of things in my life that needed cleaning up so that I could develop a more Christlike character and be ready for His coming. At the same time, Allan and I began to experience an intense time of trouble (see chapter 13). Why is it that we tend to go about our own merry way until tough times hit and it's only when we realize we can't make it by ourselves that we turn our whole lives over to Christ?

The more I grew spiritually, the more I began to experience incredible answers to prayer. One of the most unbelievable happened in September of 1994. It was a beautiful fall day. I got up early so I could go with Allan to Knoxville, drop him off at work, and then go on to North Carolina to get a truckload of apples.

On our way to Knoxville, I read to Allan out of a devotional book about the potter and the clay and the importance of being willing to be molded as clay in the hands of the potter. We read Jeremiah 18:3-6: "Then I went down to the potter's house, and there he was, making something at the wheel. And the vessel that he made of clay was marred in the hand of the potter; so he made it again into another vessel, as it seemed good to the potter to make. Then the word of the Lord came to me, saying: 'O house of Israel, can I not do with you as this potter?' " (NKJV).

We talked about how we wanted to be shaped and molded by God and of how we must live so close to Him moment by moment that we will be willing to do whatever the Holy Spirit impresses us to do. Little did we know that our desire would be realized in such a dramatic way that day.

I dropped Allan off at his office in Knoxville, did a few

things I needed to do there, and then made arrangements to meet him at 2:00 that afternoon back at his office. We could then enjoy a half-hour lunch together before I headed home.

When I left Allan's office that morning, I had just enough time to drive to Carolina and get the apples. I had a wonderful trip through the mountains, which were beginning to sport their fall colors. I listened to a tape by Steve and Annie Chapman. I just praised God as I drove. Now, as I look back, I see how God was preparing me for what would occur that afternoon.

When I arrived in Carolina, they told me that the apples were not yet ready. That threw me off schedule by about forty-five minutes. As I started driving home, I thought, *I'm going to miss lunch with Allan anyway, so why not stop and get a bean burrito, since I'm so hungry?* But as I started to cross the interstate, I missed my exit and instead headed back toward Knoxville. Talking to myself, I chided, *What's wrong? Why didn't you stop, Jill? You're hungry.* But I kept going up the interstate, singing and praying.

As I drove along, I remember reaching over to the empty seat beside me and saying, "I'm so glad I have an angel with me," and proceeded to talk to my guardian angel, saying, "I wonder, are you a him—or a her?" (I found out later that angels have no gender.) As I talked to my guardian angel, I said, "It would be nice if I could see you, but maybe today is not the day. There was a time in my life, steeped in superstitions as I was, that you would have scared me to death if you would have appeared, but now I'd really like that to happen some time."

I realize that only a sanguine could carry on such an animated conversation with an invisible guardian angel! But I was having a wonderful time. I needed to go to the restroom and intended to stop at the next rest stop, but before I realized what I'd done, I passed it. I just couldn't seem to get off the interstate. I chided myself again, *What's wrong with you, Jill? You're not only hungry, but you are miserable because you have to go, and then you didn't get off!* I decided I had better speed up to make it to another restroom. It was then that I noticed I would soon be needing gas.

As I was driving near Sevierville, Tennessee, in the middle lane, going seventy miles an hour with a bright red car on my right, a semitruck on my left, and a banana left over from breakfast in one hand, suddenly I heard a loud noise and almost lost control of the truck. I threw the banana down, quickly grabbed the wheel with both hands, and cried out, "God, help me!"

Sensing the seriousness of the moment, the truck whizzed on by, and the car backed off, seeing I was in danger. I realized I must have had a blowout. Somehow, I got over to the right-hand lane and off the interstate onto the gravel berm, and the little red car, instead of stopping to help me, flew past. I thought, *Lord, what am I doing here? I'm starved, I don't have any gas, and I still haven't taken care of my needs?* I looked at the tire—it was in shreds. "Help me not to cry," I prayed. "Help me to know what to do." Then, as I was getting the jack out, I added, "And please, Lord, send someone to help me!"

Just then, out of the corner of my eye, I saw another red

car. I thought, *The other red car passed me. Where did this one come from?* The red car continued down the bank, across the ditch, and I thought, *Oh, they're coming to help me!* As I started back around the truck to check it out, I looked again and saw that there was a man in the red car, and as he got closer, I could tell it was Allan. He stuck his head out the window and said in a very kind, chivalrous manner, "Lady, do you need some help?"

"Oh, my knight in shining armor!" I exclaimed. "I just asked God to send me a helper, but I didn't realize He'd send you!" I looked at my watch. It said two o'clock—the exact time Allan and I had arranged to meet at his office! I said, "Oh, Allan, God meant for us to meet here and not at your office."

(Allan) I had meant to go to the nursing home in Sevierville and get back by the appointed time, but I had a meeting all morning at the office and was detained. As soon as the meeting was over, I grabbed a company car, rushed to the nursing home, made a quick visit, and was heading back to the interstate, when I realized I was about out of gas. I got gas, and just as I was pulling onto the overpass, out of the corner of my eye I saw a little white truck that looked familiar going under the bridge. I began to look for it on the other side of the bridge, but I didn't see it come out. So as I pulled onto the on ramp, I continued to look for it.

Finally, I noticed it just past the bridge, and beside it was a woman in a familiar denim skirt and red blouse looking at the right front tire. Ignoring the possibility of getting stuck, I pulled down over the bank, drove along the grassy center area, and turned the car so I could straddle and cross the ditch. Just as I pulled up and said, "Lady, do you need some help?" Jill began to cry.

I have gone by that spot hundreds of times. There was a window of time of not more than three seconds for me to see the truck, or I would have missed it entirely.

(Jill) It was then that I understood why I had not stopped at Taco Bell or the rest area. God had arranged a two o'clock meeting place for Allan and me, and I couldn't be late—not even three seconds late (which is really something for me)! Who knows, it might have been my guardian angel sitting next to me who stepped on my gas pedal and steered me straight ahead when I intended to make those two stops. Someday I'm going to ask!

If Allan and I had to choose one thing that has meant the most to us in our spiritual journey, it would have to be the specialness of the Sabbath. I had gone to Sunday school all my life, but after church and Sunday dinner, life pretty much resumed its normal pace. Not so for those who live an Adventist lifestyle. Adventists keep holy twenty-four hours each week, as God instructed in the fourth commandment: "Remember the Sabbath day, to keep it holy" (Exodus 20:8, NKJV). Because the Bible records that the evening and the morning make up the days of creation, Adventists keep the Sabbath day holy as the Jews have done for thousands of years, from sundown Friday night to sundown Sabbath evening (see Genesis 1).

If you have never kept the Sabbath day holy, you have no idea the incredible blessing this can be for your family. Without this commandment, which gives us permission to rest from projects, making money, housework, worry, and all the other things that occupy our time during the other six days, I think Allan would have worked himself to death. I even wonder if we would have made it as a family!

All day Friday as I'm washing clothes, cleaning house, baking bread, and preparing a special meal so we are ready for Sabbath, I can hardly wait for the sun to set so we can welcome the Sabbath. How wonderful it is to be able to leave behind all the things I haven't gotten done during the week and to not even feel guilty. What a treat to be freed from my list of things to do so I can fully concentrate on celebrating with our family and worshiping our awesome God.

Throughout the years, we've established certain rituals that help our children look forward to these sacred hours and to experience just how special God's Sabbath is. First, we light the Sabbath candles, and then we sit around the living room and sip sparkling grape or apple juice as we discuss what we learned that week, what God has done for us, and what we are most thankful for.

During our special Friday evening worship time, we study the Bible, read stories, or play games such as *Twenty Bible Questions* or board games like *Bible Scramble* or *Choices*. When the boys were younger, they enjoyed Bible charades, dressing up and acting out various Bible characters.

Friday night is also the only time during the week I play the piano. Maybe it's because "Don't Forget the Sabbath" is about the only song I can play! I love to hear Allan's beautiful voice sing with the boys,

"Don't forget the Sabbath,
The Lord our God hath blest.
Of all the week the brightest,
Of all the week the best;
It brings repose from labor,
It tells of joy divine,
Its beams of light descending,
With heavenly beauty shine."

When the boys began trumpet lessons, we encouraged Allan to pull his own dust-covered trumpet out of the closet and play with them. Now on Friday evenings our house is filled with music.

I treasure the Sabbath hours we spend together as a family. For many years it was the only time in the week the boys really got to enjoy their daddy. Perhaps that's why Sabbath is such a delight to me. It has been the stabilizing force in our lives. It is the only consistent thing in our weekly schedules. It brings regularity to our home. It allows us to stop doing the work that otherwise would never be done and enjoy ourselves for who we are, not for what we have accomplished. On Friday night, earth time stops for me and eternity starts. It's wonderful. It's fun.

After attending Sabbath School and the church service on Saturday morning, we continue our celebration of the Sabbath by having guests over for a special Sabbath dinner. We set the table with china and silver and serve a special dessert.

Allan always plans a special Sabbath afternoon activity for the boys. If the weather is good, they enjoy hiking around Indian Boundary Lake, going up the mountain to

Bullet Creek Falls or taking the trail to White Cliff, where the boys nearly give me heart failure going so close to the edge. Sometimes they join me in missionary work, such as handing out literature and visiting people.

(Allan) One Sabbath when I realized Jill would be attending a Sabbath School council meeting after lunch, I was impressed that the boys and I should go over to Miss Georgia's and play our trumpets for her, since she hadn't been able to come to church for some time. We played old familiar hymns for an hour or so. When it was time to go, tears streamed down Miss Georgia's face, and she invited us to come again. I thought little more about the incident until Jill called me at the office Monday morning with the news that Miss Georgia had died that morning. As Jonathan said, "I learned that when God tells you to do something, you do it right then." That lesson made an impact on all of us, and we started visiting and playing for other elderly people on Sabbath afternoons.

Because of Jill, my spiritual life is constantly growing. "Religion" is not nearly as important as it used to be. I'm not even sure I know all the Bible answers, as I once thought I did. But I'm beginning to know God better through the extravagant love Jill and I are enjoying. Even the concept of the Father, Son, and Holy Spirit being three in one is easier to understand as Jill and I grow closer together and feel the unity of spiritual oneness. I experience a sense of peace when I hear Jill pray aloud for me, for I know God answers her prayers. Although my faith sometimes seems weak, it is growing. If God can take Jill and me and mold our selfish, flawed individual selves into a beautiful marriage relationship where our one desire is to do His will, then I know that "With God all things are possible" (Mark 10:27).

CHAPTER

12

Couple Strength in Tempting Times

(Allan) Growing up on a farm, I've watched how cows act when they have eaten away the grass on their side of the fence. First, they start sticking their heads through the fence, sampling the tender green shoots they can reach. But if you're not careful to provide enough feed on their side, I've seen them break down the fence to get to the green grass beyond.

It's not so different in marriage. I remember the old-timers saying, "Husbands, if you feed your heifer at home, she won't have to stray."

There's truth to that—for both husbands and wives! If you fail to feed your wife the affection she needs, she's apt to roam! And, of course, the same thing can be said for wives meeting their husband's needs. If men are starved

9—L.B.L.

for admiration and their sexual needs aren't met, they are apt to wander outside the fence of marriage too.

The problem is that seldom does infidelity start with an intentional decision. Instead, the forming of psychological or physical attachments to someone other than your spouse starts so innocently that many don't realize they're breaking down the fence until it's too late and their wayward behavior has destroyed their marriage. I'm thankful that didn't happen to Jill and me—*but, for the grace of God,* it could have!

That's why I tell husbands, if your wife has broken through the fence looking for greener grass, consider the conditions she was living under. You need to learn to love her for who she is, not for what she does for you. Just because a man gets married, that doesn't mean he knows how to be loving. I'm a prime example of that. Our homes should be the place where the green grass of unconditional love and genuine affection grows so abundantly that there's no need to look elsewhere. But, unfortunately, few of us are blameless!

I'm reminded of Jesus' words to those who were condemning the woman caught in adultery: "He who is without sin among you, let him throw a stone at her first" (John 8:7, NKJV). We are all probably guilty at times of not loving our wives as we should. Our standard should be, "Husbands, love your wives, just as Christ also loved the church and gave Himself for it" (Ephesians 5:25, NKJV). When men love in that way, it's easy for their wives to submit to their love.

Then, as those guilty men slipped quietly away, notice

what Jesus said to the woman: "Neither do I condemn you; go and sin no more" (John 8:11). I think Jesus is saying that to us, as husbands and wives, today. Even though we've made mistakes, He doesn't condemn us. Instead, He forgives and challenges us to not repeat our mistakes.

I'll be honest. I haven't always loved Jill as I should have, and I almost lost her to "greener" pastures because of the way I treated her. But I'll let Jill tell the story.

(Jill) I once received a telephone call from Meridith,* who was a good friend of mine. She said that at her work was a man who was showing quite a lot of interest in her. Her own husband was very busy at his job, and she was being torn between the two of them. She knew she shouldn't be unfaithful to her husband, but at the same time, she was really beginning to have feelings for this other guy. She admitted, "I don't know what to do!"

Meridith and I were prayer partners. We'd often call and encourage each other. That's why her revelation to me was such a shock. My response was, "Wow, I can't believe you are being tempted."

When I hung up, I kept shaking my head. I kept repeating, "I can't believe she really feels that way!" I thought at the time that I would never do such a thing. I would never become involved with another guy, even if Allan weren't the perfect husband. But I learned not ever to say, "I'll never do that," because you might do it if you find yourself in a similar position—as I did a few months later. The devil can tempt you, even when you think you are strong. And it all happened so innocently! If God hadn't seen my weakness and taken this fellow out of our lives when He did, I wonder just how far I would have gone before I had come to realize that I was breaking down the fence of marriage!

A few weeks after I received this disturbing call from Meridith, Allan and I were asked by one of our friends if a nice young man could come and live with us for a while. Fred* had been a Catholic and was now a born-again Christian who had joined our church. He didn't have a job and was wanting to continue growing in his Christian faith.

At this time in our lives, Allan was working two jobs. He'd get up at 5:00 a.m. or before and wouldn't be back until late at night, so we didn't have much time together. I was home-schooling the boys, plus caring for Allan's various projects, so I had lots of work to do around our place, and I had no time to have a healthy outlet for my sanguine personality, such as socializing with girlfriends or giving Bible studies.

So we made arrangements for Fred to come and live with us. He played with the boys and helped with their schoolwork. He would cook. He would clean. It was wonderful. He did all the things I had been pushing Allan to do but that he was too busy to get done. Fred was a fun person, and we'd laugh and joke as we'd take the boys on hikes, work in the garden, or exercise together.

When Allan would ask, "How are things going?" I'd say, "Great!" because I really was enjoying Fred—but I had a funny feeling that something wasn't right. I began to wake up in the morning and look forward to doing things with him. He was easy to talk to, and we shared many things. But it was not until he made me a birthday dinner that I realized that I was beginning to have an emotional bonding to him. It was such a thoughtful thing for him to do!

I was so naive. I was thanking the Lord for this person because he was taking a lot of pressure from me with all the things I had to do, but at the same time I was playing with fire! And I was the one who had said just a few months earlier that it could never happen to me! I learned that no one is immune to feelings of attachment to someone who is kind and caring and spends a great deal of time with you.

About this time, my brother John needed someone to help him at a school in New Hampshire and asked if Fred would be interested in coming. Within a week's time, a businessman and John flew down to the Athens airport, interviewed Fred, and he flew back with them the next day.

It was not until Fred left our home that I began to realize how much I had become attached to him. It was as if God were watching out for us, knew that I was vulnerable, and took care of the situation before I had completely broken down the fence of our marriage.

(Allan) I had no idea what was happening in our home. I just knew that Jill had a new sparkle in her eyes and that life seemed to be easier for her. In a way, I was glad, because she wasn't so demanding of me. I now realize that I was the one who put Jill into this situation by being so busy that I wasn't there to meet her needs. We were trying harder at this time to communicate. But talk alone, without time together, is not enough to keep the green grass growing at home!

Jill wasn't the only naive one, however. I was just as naive when it came to relationships with women. For example,

I had no idea what a pat on the shoulder of a woman I worked with could lead to.

I was working two jobs—one at a nursing home in Sweetwater and one in Knoxville. I would go to the nursing home in Sweetwater every morning as soon as I would get up—sometimes as early as three or four o'clock—and stay until 7:30 a.m., when I would rush to Knoxville and work my regular hours. Then on my return from work, I would stop back at the nursing home and stay until eight or nine in the evening. Then I would go back for four to six hours every Sunday. I lived like this for two years. How foolish this decision was. The love of money, or the need for the security I thought money would provide, almost destroyed that which was most precious—my marriage!

During the time I was working so hard in the nursing home, one of the aides began to spend time in the administrator's office while I was there. She didn't have a happy homelife, and she would talk. I felt sorry for her, and one time I patted her shoulder as a way of saying, "I understand." One day she handed me a note. A descriptive note. An invitation. Talk about being shocked! I told her I wasn't interested in her proposition, but that didn't stop the notes. I grew frustrated and tried to make her understand, but it didn't work.

This was during the time when Jill and I were beginning to put a major effort into getting our lives put back together. We had been to Marriage Encounter six years earlier, had gone through some major ups and downs, and now, because our pastor had mentioned that I needed to make sure I wasn't crushing Jill, we had started communicating better. Both of us were trying hard to meet each other's needs—even though I was still far too busy to be the husband and father I should have been. In an attempt to spend more time together, I decided to hire our boys to do the lawn work at the nursing home so that at least on those nights when Jill brought the boys over, we could eat supper together and enjoy some family time.

When I realized that this woman was propositioning me, and when I asked her to stop and she wouldn't, I knew I had a problem. I immediately called Jill and explained the situation and asked, "Jill, what do you think I should do?"

"No problem," Jill said. "The next time I bring the boys over to mow the lawn, I'll talk to her."

Jill will never know what a burden she took from my shoulders. It's one thing to fight alone when something is threatening your marriage, but it's quite another to join forces and fight together as a team. I realized for the first time the incredible sense of security there is in couple power! If Jill would stand beside me, we could overcome this problem or any other problem the devil could throw in our paths. But the problem wasn't as simple to solve as I thought at the moment.

(Jill) After I told Allan that I would talk to this woman, I began to question my boldness. I had no idea what I would say. I just prayed that God would give me the words.

A couple of days later, when we went to the nursing home to do the mowing, I called the woman and asked, "Are you coming to work this evening? I have something to talk to you about." We waited for a while, but she never showed up.

The next day when I was home, I received a call from her. She said nervously, "I didn't sleep all night wondering what you wanted to talk to me about."

I said, "I wouldn't sleep all night either if I were doing what you are doing."

She tried to act innocent and asked, "Oh, what do you mean?"

"Well," I informed her, "I think you should understand that I am aware that you are sending letters to my husband and that he has asked you to stop. He has shared this with me and asked me if I could do something to make you understand that we want you to quit bothering us."

Her response was, "Oh, you should hate me for what I've done. You must be a Christian to be treating me so nicely." That gave me an opportunity to talk to her about our belief system. I also told her that I hoped she would get her life straightened out so she would be prepared to meet Christ some day, because the Lord was coming soon. I closed the conversation saying that I had a concern about her life and her relationship with God.

Later, when we found out that this woman was involved in spiritualism and seances, I told Allan that this reminded me of the text, "For we do not wrestle against flesh and blood, but against principalities, against powers, against the rulers of the darkness of this age, against spiritual hosts of wickedness in the heavenly places" (Ephesians 6:12, NKJV).

The woman stopped sending notes to Allan, and shortly afterward she quit work and filed for unemployment benefits, saying she had been sexually harassed. Allan attended the unemployment hearing, but she never showed up. Her request was denied because of Tennessee law.

We found out later she really quit to start a home-based business, needed start-up money, and thought she could get it through unemployment.

Allan had no idea about her accusation until he received a call from the editor of the local paper. "You have been charged with sexual harassment—do you have any comment you want to make?"

(Allan) It took me aback when the editor hit me with this accusation. "Yes, I have one comment. The charge has no basis, and you better have your facts together before you publish anything!"

The article came out in the paper. My accuser had gotten another woman to join her in her plot, so there were two who were making the accusation. The article didn't name me, but there was so much information given that if you knew anything at all about the nursing home, you would know who the accusation was against.

My first boss, a retired army colonel, had once told me, "It doesn't do any good to get into a fight with a tar baby. You may win, but you'll have tar all over you." His words came back to me in this situation. My adversary definitely fit the "tar baby" category! I felt the only thing I could do was to duck my head and let it rain. It helped to have Jill standing beside me during this time of persecution. This was a lesson I'll never forget!

Now that I look back on our life experiences, I can see how very careful a person must be to keep body, mind, and soul true to his or her companion. In Jill's case, I had no idea she was being drawn to the fellow living in our home. If I'd kept the "green grass growing" in our marriage and provided the companionship she was craving, there would have been no threat. I was the guilty one.

And as I think about the woman I patted on the back, if I'd involved Jill more in my life instead of being so busy, if I had been home talking to Jill instead of listening to the heartaches of this other woman at work, I doubt she would have propositioned me.

I'm convinced that J. Allen Peterson is right when he says in the book *The Myth of the Greener Grass* that we must burglarproof our marriages. The way to keep the thief from taking our most precious possession is to treat that most precious person like the treasure he or she is.

Alone, one becomes vulnerable. A couple, however, who are committed to their marriage and willing to share and stand together in hard times, has incredible power against whatever may threaten their marriage. I'm thankful Jill and I were far enough down our rocky road toward extravagant love that we were able to have the couple strength we needed to support and stay true to each other.

I underlined these words in Peterson's book:

> Nothing is finer, more fulfilling, indeed more sanctified, than the inviolate (not violated) marriage bed, particularly when the decision that it will remain inviolate is the conscious act of two people who share it (198).

Be faithful, stay faithful, have faith, and happiness will happen.

*Names have been changed.

13

For Richer; for Poorer

(Jill) When Allan and I were first married, I paid the bills, and everything went fine while we were in our little apartment in town. We lived simply, but we had more money than I had ever had before in my life.

Once we moved to our mobile home in the country, things became somewhat disorganized. Everything was so crowded, and I didn't have enough storage places to put things away. Plus, it took us a lot of time to keep kerosene in the lamps and carry the water for cooking and bathing, in the summer to keep ice in our ice chest since we didn't have a refrigerator, and in the winter to get wood for the wood heater.

Because of this, sometimes the bills would get misplaced. Soon after we got the phone put in, the phone bill got misplaced. I thought I had paid it. One day I needed to make a couple of calls and found that the phone didn't work. I was really disturbed, because that was my link to the world. So when Allan came home I said, "There is something wrong with the phone. Can you believe it? They ought to give better service!"

That night when we went to prayer meeting at our church in Athens, I said to Allan, "I'll call the phone company to report that our phone is out of order." When I started to complain to the phone representative about their service, the lady said, "Ma'am, you haven't paid your phone bill, so your phone was disconnected." I was mortified that I had made such a big deal out of the phone company's lack of service, when it was my own fault!

Allan was not only embarrassed, but indignant. He had grown up in a home where you paid your bills on time and your debtors could trust you. Now I had shattered his good image. So he said to me, "If you can't keep the bills paid, I'll just do it myself," and he took all the bills and the checkbook away from me.

I remember saying, "I really don't care. Let him pay the bills if he wants to"—but I really did care. It was a terrible blow to my self-esteem. I was frustrated, because I wanted so badly to be organized and not make those kinds of mistakes. And in spite of my good intentions, I had blown it.

Allan kept the bills paid, but with all the projects he had going, he got behind in reconciling the bank statements. After two years of not balancing the checkbook, he brought me a big box with all the bank statements and all the canceled checks and asked me if I would help him organize our financial matters.

I took this as a challenge. I said to myself, "I can do it." We didn't have electricity for a calculator, so I took the box over to a friend's house and worked for weeks trying to balance it. Finally, I gave up and just closed that account and started a new one.

It wasn't long, however, until Allan decided he would take over paying the household bills again. I'm sure he thought he was helping me, because I was pregnant at the time and would soon be busy with a baby. But the checkbook had become my symbol of self-worth, and when he grabbed it back, it hurt me. I didn't argue with him, but after a while, he got busy again, and he gave it back to me. It was like a seesaw, back and forth, until we went to Marriage Encounter and Allan learned how important it was to share responsibilities. He asked me if I'd like to take over the checkbook. I said Yes. I then went to a friend who showed me a simple way to keep things organized and balanced. Once I knew exactly what to do, I was able to keep the household financial records of our family without any problem. If only Allan, who had academic training in financial matters, would have taken some time to show me how to do this years before!

Although I complained that Allan's projects weren't really moneymakers if you counted in all my time, sweat, and tears, he had always had a reasonable profit. Then came our own "Black Monday," when we almost lost everything we had.

(Allan) I had started working in Knoxville, and I was making more money and wanted to find a way to invest in something that would be financially rewarding.

One afternoon I decided to take off work and spend some time with my family. Jill was home-schooling and needed to take the boys to their trumpet lessons in Collegedale, and I had some errands to run in nearby Chattanooga. Whenever Jill was in Collegedale, she would stop at the produce market to buy fresh fruits and vegetables. This time when we went in, the owner of the store was there and began to talk with me. We shared things in common, and when he heard that I was an administrator, he said, "Man, I need someone like you to join me and handle the administration of this business." I questioned the feasibility of doing this, because of the distance—over an hour from our home—and how much involvement it would take. I wondered if this was the right investment to make with the money we had been saving. The young man assured me that it would not take on-site, day-to-day administration, but only someone on a weekly or monthly basis to come down and make sure things were in order.

As I got back into the car, I was somewhat excited about the possibility of this new produce market and landscaping business venture. But I felt prompted to ask, "Jill, do you think this is something we ought to do?" We both concluded, "Let's pray about it." Our daily petition was "Lord, help us to make a wise decision. What is Your will for our lives?" In addition to praying, I got as much information as I could about the business. I thought I had thoroughly investigated the financial condition of the business, but, unfortunately, this man withheld the fact that there were back taxes and that personal loans were owed.

The ironic thing is that this was the one project Jill and I had thoroughly discussed between the two of us, and we had each prayed about it earnestly. After much consideration, it seemed that all the doors were opened for us to go for it, so we signed the necessary papers to form a partnership.

Not long after that, we got a call from one of the workers saying that the market doors had been padlocked by the IRS. No one could get into the building until a certain portion of the taxes due had been paid. I was shocked! For a person like me who prided myself on paying my debts, this discovery was a terrible blow to my ego.

We then found out that the man we had gone into partnership with was a big talker but didn't have a dime. Several months afterward, he disappeared, leaving us with the full responsibility for the market's financial debt. We paid the taxes we knew were due, but then a few months later, another tax bill from several years earlier arrived. This one was for an exorbitant amount because of the accumulated penalties. I was devastated. We had figured that with the market business, we could have our home paid off in one year and then be debt-free. Instead, this investment was plunging us toward financial ruin. Bankruptcy for us was not an option. We had always been honorable about paying our debts, and we would somehow survive this financial disaster. We sold off assets, refinanced our home, and cashed in our savings, and throughout the next few years lost over $80,000 on this business venture.

This was the first time, regardless of how hard I worked, that I couldn't make a success of something. The more I poured into the business, the more bills came in from un-known sources, including personal loans this fellow had arranged from people I knew and whom I considered my friends. Finally, the only option we had was to close the doors.

(Jill) I once laughed when I heard the jingle:

> That money talks, I'll not deny,
> I heard it once—it said goodbye!

But the money we lost on the market was no laughing matter. It was the worst nightmare I could have imagined. I had gone through a lot of traumatic experiences with Allan, but this topped them all. I actually thought that, although I'm strong, this would do me in.

I dreaded going to the post office to get the mail for fear of receiving another IRS notice. At first we had tried to let others manage the business. But it didn't take us long to realize that one of us had to be there or things were mis-managed or stolen.

When I saw the dilemma we were in, I was eager to try and help Allan, because this was the one venture we had agreed upon together. Yet on the inside, I was angry, be-cause God had not closed the door. Why had He allowed us to get into this big mess? I kept asking, "Why, Lord? What are we going to learn from this?" Since Allan still had his demanding job in Knoxville about an hour or so north of our home, he wasn't able to supervise the busi-ness in Collegedale, which was about the same distance south. So I took over that job. As soon as Allan left in the morning, I'd drive to Collegedale with the boys, whom I was still home-schooling. As my responsibilities mounted, I didn't even have time to go home at night, so I found a place for the boys and me to stay in Collegedale during the week, and then we'd go home to be with Allan on the weekends.

I had many lessons to learn. I had never owned a business before. Suddenly I had to deal with all the problems that go along with one. All my life I had tried hard to avoid conflict, and now I even had to fire someone. It was a very painful experience.

The lawn-mowing crew quit, and to get the help I needed, I had to go to Englewood to round up two neighbors who needed work. Since they didn't have transportation, I had to take them to the job sites, supervise, and help in the mowing. I hated to leave our little boys sitting on the back bench in the produce market doing schoolwork assignments while I had to be out working in the hot sun with the landscaping crew.

In addition, the stress of trying to satisfy unreasonable people was hard on me. One day a lady called, complaining that we had mowed her lawn in the wrong direction. She wanted us to go up and down instead of crossways. I couldn't believe it. I had worked so hard on her lawn I nearly had a sun stroke. And as we left the site, I had even looked back to inspect our work and commented, "Man, doesn't that look beautiful!" And now this complaint! Can you believe it—she wanted us to do it over?

I was so exhausted that I nearly collapsed in the office when her irate call came in. I told my co-worker that I

10—L.B.L.

didn't have the energy to return and to just give the lady her money back and apologize for not doing it the right way! The lady took back her money and was very rude to us. She looked rich, but she had a poor attitude when it came to people who were trying to provide a service to her! This really hurt me after I had tried so hard to please her.

Throughout all these trials, the thought of what Jesus might say kept coming back to me. "You are paying a debt you don't owe, but I paid a debt for you that I didn't owe!" That thought sustained me through the next few months. I kept praying, "Lord, if You have something else to teach us through this, just help us to learn it quickly!"

We struggled for two years, from 1987 to 1989, to make the market venture a success before we gave up.

At the time, not only was I struggling with what God was trying to teach us but Allan was forced to reprioritize his life goals. One day his non-Christian boss in Knoxville sat down and asked Allan how things were going. Allan replied, "I have learned a lesson from the market business. When everything was going well in my life, money was becoming more important to me than anything else. Now I have rearranged my priorities. God is first. Family is second. And business is third."

It was not only difficult trying to teach the boys the remainder of that school year while struggling with the business, but my health was deteriorating because of thyroid trouble, fibrocystic growths, and hormone problems. I think my body was telling me "You can't go on. The stress is too much." Emotionally, I was falling apart, and I believed that I was near a nervous breakdown.

During this process, the fellow in charge of the landscaping part of our business was found hanging from a tree in his backyard. We had just gone to his wedding a year earlier. He was such a nice-looking young man, but he just couldn't handle it when creditors began hounding him. I mourned his senseless death.

About this time, Allan also became the administrator of the nursing home in Sweetwater. He figured that with this extra job he could earn some more money to pay the market debt. It helped some, but it also increased our stress. To add to this, an aide at the nursing home started chasing Allan and let it be known that she was praying that since I was so physically weak, I would die so she could have him. Then she ended up accusing him of sexual harassment! This is the last thing we needed in our lives!

At the same time, we had a personality clash with the pastor of our church and were treated so unkindly by him that we finally chose to go to a church in Hixson, which was over an hour from our home. We grieved over this decision, because our friends for fifteen years, and our support group, had been made up of members of the church we were leaving.

Just before we got into the market business and all these other things happened to us, I had prayed to be one of the 144,000 and for God to do whatever was necessary to prepare us for the privilege of being in this elite group. I had no idea our time of trouble would come so quickly! Now I found myself pleading, "Lord, I feel like Moses in the wilderness. I feel like no one wants me." I remember staying up all night in prayer. I kept trying to see God's hand in all this chaos:

- Our business was failing and plummeting us into massive debt.
- We had been rejected by some in our church of fifteen years.
- I was physically and emotionally falling apart, with various physical ailments and pain.
- A woman was chasing my husband, threatening our marriage.
- And Allan and I were busier than we had ever been in our lives, which made it impossible to spend much time together.

In addition, my brother, who was my friend and spiritual support, who had always lived close, moved to New Hampshire, over a thousand miles away. This left me with more responsibility for my mother, who at the time was being abused in her marriage. I was thrilled when my mother decided to become a Seventh-day Adventist, but this added to the stress, since her husband threatened her life if she were to go ahead with her plans. She didn't let this stop her, but when I took her home after her baptism, he again threatened and insisted that I take her away and never bring her back.

It seemed that one thing after another kept falling in on us. I just prayed that nothing more tragic would occur. I thought of the most awful thing that could happen and prayed, "Lord, don't let my kids die." I was feeling so persecuted that I felt I couldn't go on.

Through it all, there were some bright spots. A pastor friend encouraged us and also insisted on giving us money for groceries when he heard about our financial crisis. I wept. I knew then what it was like to be in need, totally broke, with no place to turn. The boys and I rejoiced as we went to the grocery store and bought some fruit and vegetables that we needed. Because we nearly lost everything we had, I'll forever look differently on people who are hit with hard times.

Another blessing that came to us at this time was that the boys and I were invited to join the Pathfinder Club at the McDonald church, which was close to Collegedale. It was a nice outlet. There were friends there who prayed with us and supported us through this time of crisis. Our family grew spiritually through the association of the support system of that church. The bitter taste in our mouths because of the cruel way we had been treated was replaced with the sweetness we experienced in this fellowship.

Our time of financial trouble taught us that money is not as important to our family as our relationship with God. Even in the darkest moments, God cares and can provide the help and support we need. At such times, I find the words of David comforting:

> Yea, though I walk through the valley of the shadow of death,
>   I will fear no evil;
>   For You are with me;
>   Your rod and Your staff, they comfort me.

You prepare a table before me in the presence of
my enemies;
You anoint my head with oil;
My cup runs over.
Surely goodness and mercy shall follow me
All the days of my life;
And I will dwell in the house of the Lord Forever
(Psalm 23: 4-6, NKJV).

I thought I couldn't go on, but I was wrong. God never allows us to bear more than we are able, and in a way, it is an honor that God was able to trust us with so much. Although, for us personally, the market was a financial disaster, it did not destroy us. If we had not been pulled into that business at that particular moment, everyone who had been owed money, from the friends who had loaned to the IRS, would have lost what was due them. But we were chosen in a way as the redeemer to make it right. It did not crush us. We have been able to pay, through hard work and the blessings of the Lord, and are indeed spiritually stronger because of it.

The message that was hammered into me during this financial time of trouble was best said in the words of a song: "I owed a debt I couldn't pay. He paid a debt He didn't owe. Christ Jesus paid it all."

(Allan) My experience with the market made me very, very conservative from a financial standpoint. It taught me to be far more cautious in business dealings and not to be so trusting of others. I see now that people sometimes take advantage of others in order to personally benefit.

If anything, I blame myself for being so trusting. But all was not lost. I was the one who benefited from the many lessons to be learned from this financial disaster. You don't learn anything in life when you run away, as my partner did. I hold no grudges. Who knows—someday he may realize what he did and make it right.

All of us have a certain amount of time and money, but few have both in liberal amounts. Many people spend all their time in pursuit of money and lose sight of the priorities that have more lasting value, such as family and God. I've also noticed that some who have money are obnoxious and take advantage of others. However, I have decided that if that is the price money requires, I don't want it. My goal is to provide for my family, to help others in need, and to be of service to mankind. I only want the amount of money the Lord can trust me with to fulfill those goals.

CHAPTER

14

Opening Doors of Possibility

(**Allan**) I had worked for years trying to introduce discipline into Jill's life so she could reach her full potential. Growing up with organization and hard work, our family had achieved numerous difficult accomplishments, and I wanted the same for us, but I couldn't do it alone.

Finally, I came to realize that what I was doing wasn't working. So I decided to let go of my ideas of what Jill should be doing, such as having a neat and orderly house, fixing decent food to eat, and being on time to appointments—and turn the job over to God.

In doing so, I began to recognize Jill's natural, God-given talents and intelligence. Instead of being critical and negative about those things she didn't do well, I began to be her talent scout, matching needs with her gifts and strengths. If she showed an interest in something—such as going back to school or speaking for church—I began encouraging her to go for it. I was so successful and, initially, Jill so hesitant, that she in embarrassment chided me for being so bold as to suggest she could do these things. I obviously had a lot of building up to do after all those years of tearing her down.

Once I made the decision to love her unconditionally, just because she existed and not for what she did, my observational skills refocused. Instead of looking for things to criticize, I began to look for situations to star Jill. Mom had always said, "You can find good in everyone—with some you just have to look a little longer." Because Jill excelled in areas I had not previously valued, I had ignored her strengths and instead I had focused all my attention on areas I thought were important and where I thought she needed to improve.

Now I redoubled my efforts to support and encourage her in her areas of strength—yet did not push her beyond what she really wanted to do. I became her helpmate, not her controller. I became her supporter, not her criticizer. I became her cheerleader, not her accuser.

I knew Jill had gifts: she has excellent people skills—everyone loves her and enjoys being around her, because she makes them feel important. She is a natural-born speaker—she can spontaneously get up and speak with enthusiasm and humor about her experiences in life, and she is a fearless Christian witness, sharing Christ and her testimony with anyone who shows a need or an interest.

Now my challenge was to recognize Jill's natural gifts

and take a supportive role, using my gifts to complement hers. I began to see the exponential effects of such an approach to marriage. Two, working together as a united team, could accomplish far more than just the sum of one plus one.

And just about the time I was falling in love once again with Jill and rethinking my approach to her, Kay Kuzma walked into our lives.

(Jill) It happened in 1992 at a Sabbath afternoon program at Wildwood Institute, in Georgia. We decided to drive over to Wildwood to see my brother, who was attending meetings there. We had no idea we would run into Kay. We almost left before the afternoon meeting, but since the boys were having fun playing outside, we decided to stay to hear the Polish singers, and what happened next was what I consider a divine appointment. Kay walked in. I couldn't believe it, since I had just called her a few days before about speaking in our church, and she had said she was too busy. But the real shock came when I went up to talk to her after the program, and as soon as I had reminded her of my name, she blurted, "I need you to be me!"

"What do you mean?" I asked.

"I need help!" she explained, telling me that she had so many speaking appointments that she needed someone to take the appointments she couldn't. I was shocked she was asking me! I had no qualifications. But just then Allan walked up and totally embarrassed me by saying, "Jill is an excellent speaker. She could do a great job."

I said, "Allan," as I poked him in the ribs and then whispered, "What are you talking about? You have no idea what she is saying to me."

But that didn't stop him. "I know she can do it." All I could say was "I need to pray about this!"

On the way home, when we told the boys what had happened, they said, "Sure, Mom, you've had lots of practice. You'd make a good preacher."

My only comment was "I need to pray about this."

"But," Allan said, "you've already prayed about it."

Then I remembered what Allan was referring to—the day in the park. But to understand what happened in the park, you have to go back to the beginning of our marriage, when Allan was so controlling of me. He made me feel stupid. He showed no interest in helping me find a way to go back to school. He didn't even think I had the skills to pay the bills. I tried to buy his love by becoming Miss Homemaker, but the job wasn't a good match, and when all I got was more criticism, I finally just became the silent partner, doing whatever I could to avoid making him angry so that he wouldn't criticize me.

During these years, my identity got mixed up with Allan's. I was Allan's wife—not Jill Kennedy. If Allan was a success, I got the crumbs, and that's pretty much the way I lived for far too many years. Then came Marriage Encounter—and six years later our pastor, who noticed that the sparkle had faded from my eyes and cared enough to confront Allan with, "Allan, you have a precious flower in Jill. Just make sure you don't crush her!"

So when Allan began to love me for who I was, not for what I did, and when he began to encourage me to become my own person, I had a long way to go to resurrect the self-confident Jill Kennedy of my high-school years. I had been so conditioned that I was stupid and couldn't do anything worthwhile that I was afraid to try. I think I felt a lot like Moses did after wandering in the wilderness for forty years. I was not only slow of speech but lacking in just about every other skill needed to do anything worthwhile in this world.

Slowly, I began to see that my true value was in Jesus Christ. Although I didn't have self-confidence, I was beginning to have God-confidence. I was encouraged when I read something published in the *Signs of the Times*, September 9, 1886: "In order to be a good wife it is not necessary that a woman's nature should be utterly merged in that of her husband. It is not the design of the Creator that our individuality should be lost in another's."

Allan kept telling me that I had a lot to offer, but I didn't know what. I thought I might go back to school, but then I began to have physical problems. I thought that maybe Allan would be disappointed in me for not being able to do the things I used to do or for not going on to school, but instead, he started bringing me red roses. He had so conditioned me during the early years of our marriage not to spend money foolishly that when he brought me that first bouquet of roses, I said without thinking, "Oh, Allan, you spent so much money! You shouldn't have done that." He was sorry for what he had done to me over the years, and he was trying hard to make it up.

Many times in my life I have run ahead of the Lord, and I have found myself in a big mess, so I began praying earnestly for the Lord to give me some direction.

One Sabbath I got up and shared during the Personal Ministries time at church. Someone said, when I had finished, "We should just end the service right now." I was surprised others could be blessed by what I said. The pastor started encouraging me. Another person said, "You should be a minister!" I loved ministry, but the thought of going back to school when I believed Jesus' coming was soon made me pray, "Lord, I don't want to be tied up in school if You need me to be witnessing right now. But if not, I'll go back to school and discipline myself—if that's what You want me to do."

I was walking and praying in the park one day when I remembered the time my sister-in-law, Linda, and I had gone to the flea market to witness. She played her guitar and sang, and soon we had a whole crowd around us. I began handing out books and pamphlets, and we spent the day giving Bible studies. "Lord," I prayed, "that day at the flea market was really fun. Maybe I should go into the ministry." All of a sudden, I got excited and said, "Lord, just give me a street corner, and I'll tell the people about You and how You have worked in our lives, because You have changed us. You are working out Your will for us."

It was this experience Allan was referring to when he said, "You've already prayed about it."

That next Tuesday, I met with Kay. She gave me every video- and audio-tape she had ever made, every book she'd written, and all her handouts. She asked me to become familiar with her materials so that when people asked for various presentations, I would be able to do them.

I began reading, listening, taking notes, and practicing.

A few weeks later I got a message on the answering machine. "Jill, will you do a camp meeting for me?" As I listened to that message, I said, "Camp meeting? Lord, I didn't ask You for a camp meeting. I just asked You for a street corner!" I shook my head and wondered, *Is this possible?*

I said Yes, but all those years that I had looked to Allan as the competent one in our family made me afraid to go without him. When I asked him, he said, "Sure, Jill, I'll go with you. We can do it together. I'll support you and help you."

We got our picture taken for the camp meeting brochure and prepared all our talks. Then at the last minute, Allan's boss said, "Allan, you can't go. Someone else in management is off that same week, and we need you here."

I felt as if I'd just been thrown into the middle of a lake and had either to sink or swim. I decided to swim. We quickly got another picture taken, and it was now just "Jill Kennedy." I was afraid. "Oh, Allan," I said, "what will I do?" He encouraged me, "You can do it!"

My family and friends rallied around me. My pastor allowed me to present the church services for a whole month so I could practice the talks I would be giving at the main camp-meeting sessions. The congregation was so supportive. It was just like one big happy family. They had seen Allan and me struggling in our marriage, they had seen the light go out in my eyes, and now they were witnessing a resurrection. There was much rejoicing as they noticed how kind and loving Allan was to me. As I left on the plane, I could hear their words of encouragement ringing in my ears, "Jill, you can do it. You can do it." I am a living example of that self-fulfilling prophecy. As others began treating me as if I had the potential to do this work, I began to stretch to meet their expectations.

On top of everything else, after all the videotape watching, all the note-taking, and all the practicing, Kay handed me the handouts for each of the five afternoon sessions for the parenting seminar. I said, "Wow, what is this stuff? This is not what I've been watching. This is foreign to me. What are the answers to all these questions? I can't go down there and show them this if I don't even know the answers." I prayed, and God gave me the wisdom to know which books to take along so I could find all the answers.

As it turned out, this experience was the best thing that could have ever happened to me for my healing and recovery at this time. I didn't like flying, and I had to fly to New Orleans with only myself and God. I took my journal along, and I recorded how God led me every step of the way. He gave me peace about flying, courage to go alone, and the God-confidence I needed to face the unknown.

So began my "street-corner" ministry.

(Allan) I was really proud of Jill. The boys and I rallied around her and were amazed at how God answered prayers so dramatically. There could be no doubt about her calling. We began traveling with her to such interesting places as Nassau, Guadeloupe, New York City, British Columbia, and Toronto and blending our talents with Jill's. I often joined her in presenting, and the boys and I would take our trumpets along and provide special music.

Jill has always been a dreamer, and one of the things she has been talking about since 1991 was for me to quit my job and go into full-time ministry. I knew that was impossible. But Jill and the Lord have such a special relationship that when Jill starts praying for something, watch out!

(Jill) God could not have told Allan to just "get up and go" as He did Abraham of old. He had to prepare him little by little in very obvious ways. Miracle upon miracle happened in our lives, but all this wasn't enough to move Allan in the direction I'll admit I was praying he would move. I didn't want to force or manipulate. If Allan ever chose to join me in full-time ministry, it would have to be between him and the Lord.

Allan has always had a strong sense of responsibility to provide for his family. Over the past nine years that Allan has worked in Knoxville, he has put the company first. It meant long hours away from the family and at times attending social functions where there was drinking and inappropriate behavior. If Allan didn't attend, people would wonder if he was being loyal to the company. At times Allan felt that his boss berated him in front of other employees, accusing him of disloyalty, stealing company time, or questioning decisions. He felt controlled and verbally abused. The job, although providing financially for our family, was robbing Allan of his self-worth and dignity.

When I was asked to go to that first camp meeting, Allan began to see God working, and even though His voice was faint, Allan heard the call to ministry for me. But the call has not been that direct for Allan.

(Allan) Part ownership in the company I worked for gave me security. It was my treasure that for a long time I wasn't willing to give up.

Ever since Jill began speaking, I had recognized that Jill had a natural gift. As I started speaking with her, I began to notice that we had a story to tell. Others were blessed. But I had a job in Knoxville that demanded my full-time attention.

Jill kept wanting me to go with her on more of her speaking appointments, but with job responsibilities, I only had a certain amount of free time.

Then things at work began to be more and more tense. Communication had broken down and although confrontations were less frequent, they were more pronounced.

Finally, I began to realize that I was not being effective, and I questioned whether I was needed or wanted.

Slowly, the Lord began impressing me with some unsettling thoughts. I began to realize that a lot of preparation had gone into bringing me to this point in my life. Truly, God was leading. If I sold certain cars, we would be out of debt. We had money for the boys' college in my retirement accounts if we needed to use them. An uncle had moved near us and would help provide security if the boys wanted to stay home while Jill and I traveled to various locations to give seminars. Our speaking appointments were well received and increasing. Plus, we had been given the opportunity to take training to become facilitators of the Life Skills Seminars, and this could provide a living. We could even coordinate Life Skills through Dr. Kay Kuzma's Family Matters organization and assist her with that ministry. But still, I was cautious.

Faye—a trusted friend at work—and I talked several times, discussing my options. I had a hard time letting go

11—L.B.L.

and trusting that my family would be provided for. One day Faye confronted me: "How could you stay here when you have such clear leading from God to do ministry?" Finally I had to admit that the weight of evidence was unmistakably in support of my joining Jill in ministry. I was beginning to think Faye was right when she said, "You'll trade a living for a life!"

(Jill) While Allan and Faye were having this discussion, I was at home walking in the mountains and praying that God would impress upon us both what Allan should do. For four years I had wanted Allan to quit his job, step out in faith, and start a family ministry with me. But I didn't want to run ahead of God—or Allan. I had done this in the past. I knew that this one time I wanted to walk beside Allan, regardless of how much time it would take him to make a decision. I wanted this to be a decision based on Allan's Holy Spirit–inspired reasoning and not merely my emotions.

While I was walking and praying, wondering if we could make it financially, the thought came to me, *Why are you concerned about your needs? Remember, I'm coming soon, and the main goal in life is to be ready with your family and to help others to know Christ and be ready for His coming.* It was almost as if God were saying, "Now is the time—get with it!"

There was such a peace that came over me. Why had I been so anxious about what I would eat and wear and the necessities of life? If God has said He would provide for our needs, He would!

For the last few days Allan had been asking me, "Should

I quit my job? Should I do this?"

I kept telling him, "Allan, I can't tell you what you should do." I wanted God to speak *directly* to Allan and not to speak to Allan through me. Or if God wanted me to take a stand and share with Allan the strong impression I had that now was the time for us to go into full-time ministry, I prayed that He would give me the courage to speak up and not revert back to my past fear that if I spoke up, Allan would not listen and reject my ideas.

Things came to a head on May 22 at about 4:00 a.m. I could hear Allan tossing in bed. Finally, he said, "Are you awake?"

"Yeah, are you awake too?"

"I can't sleep."

Then he said, "You know, this is really scary. But I'm going to do it."

When he said those words, I realized for the first time how difficult this decision had been for him. Instead of being impulsive like me, Allan was the kind who had to make sure everything was considered before stepping out. Now, even though he didn't know how deep the water was, he was going to take the plunge.

All at once I had an understanding of the emotional turmoil that had been going on inside him. Before, I had thought he was weak not to make the decision to get out of this abusive job. Now I saw that it wasn't weakness but rather his dedication to being a good provider. He kept having flashbacks of the market business we had gotten into where we almost lost everything we had—our home, our savings, our security. We had thought God had led us to that business, yet what a financial disaster! Allan didn't want us to go through that again. That's why this decision was even more scary for him.

My past experience didn't help either. I had gone through nine years or so of verbal abuse from Allan. During that time, I thought I was coping by just stuffing my feelings. But what I was really doing was dying inside. Now, Allan was dying inside—himself the victim of control. He asked for my understanding. "Jill, I'm feeling just as you felt when I said terrible things to you. I'm so sorry I did that to you."

His reminder of those awful days could have caused me to revert and let those past hurts surface and seek self-righteous revenge! I was tempted to lash out and say, "What goes around, comes around." But I had to bury the past and feel with and for Allan without our past garbage ruining the moment.

Because I made the decision to love Allan in spite of the past, there was a special closeness we felt as we prayed together before he left for work that morning. We were in this together, and I knew Allan had, with God, made the right decision. For the first time in years, I felt the fresh air of possibility blowing through a wide-open door.

CHAPTER

15

Breaking the Alabaster Box of Love

(**Allan**) It's been a rocky road that Jill and I have traveled to come finally to the reality that giving is far better than getting. The self-fulfilling prophecy is real. You've heard the saying, "Treat her like a thoroughbred, and you'll never have a nag"? It's true.

At first I concentrated on my unmet needs and schemed methods to have them filled. Or I demanded my "rights." And in so doing, I became the controller and Jill the controlled. Instead of responding in love, Jill tried to please me out of feared rejection. I lost her respect and admiration, the sparkle in her eyes disappeared, and her smile faded. My selfishness destroyed the very essence of the Jill with whom I had fallen in love.

In retrospect, I must admit that I had no idea with what

love and great commitment my needs would be met once I stopped selfishly focusing on them and instead began focusing on unselfishly meeting Jill's needs. The imagination, thoughtfulness, and creativity Jill uses to express her love and commitment to me never cease to amaze me. Let me just give you an example of what I mean.

On our twentieth wedding anniversary, Jill called me at work and said, "I have a special surprise for you. I'm coming to pick you up at work today." What I didn't know is that I was about to be kidnapped—and that my whole office staff was in on it. My secretary told me I needed to leave early so I could visit a nursing home on my way home.

With a sparkle in her eyes, Jill picked me up and turned east toward downtown Knoxville. As she passed the road to the nursing home without turning off, I began to become suspicious. I said, "Wait, wait, you missed the turn-off." With a big smile, she said, "I told you I had a surprise for you," and kept driving.

Now, for a man who is usually in control, it wasn't easy to sit back and relax and wait to see what Jill had up her sleeve. But I did!

She drove on for a few more miles and then turned off on the James White Parkway and pulled up to the Hyatt Regency, where we had honeymooned twenty years before. I'll admit that it was a little strange going into a hotel with no luggage. I wondered if anyone would believe me if, in the middle of the afternoon, I tried to explain to them that I was with my wife!

Jill took me up to the room she had arranged for us. She had everything we needed for a romantic time together, including a bottle of sparkling grape juice!

Just as we were getting comfortable, the phone rang. It was room service, wondering if they could bring us a complementary bottle of wine for our anniversary celebration. We turned down the wine but graciously accepted another bottle of sparkling juice, complete with goblets. Later, Jill took me out to dinner at a romantic little restaurant, and we enjoyed long, lingering glances—as we once had at Shoney's during the early days of our courtship.

Everything was great until I got to work the next morning, when every girl in the office, with a smile, asked me how the afternoon had gone. It then dawned on me that Jill had solicited the help of the entire office staff in order to get me out of the office in the middle of the afternoon. I'm afraid my cheeks turned pink!

Several days later, one of the single girls came up to me and said, "I hope that when I get married, my husband loves me as much as you love Jill and that my children grow up to be as nice as your two boys." If only she had known the rocky road we had traveled before we finally discovered extravagant love.

(Jill) Once I began to realize how much fun it was to meet Allan's sexual needs, I delighted in surprising him with crazy ideas. One week when we hadn't had any time together, I called Allan on his car phone as he was traveling home from Knoxville. I had a class that night, so it would be late when we'd finally see each other, and I was feeling a little neglected and was tempted to complain, "Why don't you ever spend any time with me?" Instead, I decided to tease him a little. On an impulse, I asked him what he planned to do that evening. He gave me a whole list of things. I told him I'd make it worth his while if he didn't do what he planned and instead would meet me in the parking lot at the local high school, where my Cleveland State Community College class was to be held. I said I'd be in the van.

(Allan) I had no idea what Jill was up to as I drove up beside the van. She jumped out with her eyes dancing and, as the spider said to the fly, said, "Come in!" She had made the bed and pulled the curtains. Her spontaneous plan and the unusual setting led to one of our most enjoyable evenings ever!

(Jill) I would never have done that in the early years— or during all those lost years when I didn't understand how fun and exciting married sex could be. But I give Allan the credit for finding it out in me. I would have no desire to pleasure him if it weren't for the way he shows me throughout the day just how much I'm loved.

An early love note that he wrote on one of his business cards said,

> "Dear Jewel of mine,
> I looked a long time before I found you.
> Afterward I wondered if I had found what I was looking for.
> I have found that woman of great value mentioned in Proverbs 31:10-31,
> And each day I thank God for you.
> Allan

Here's a more recent love letter, dated December 14, 1995, which I read as I was flying to Washington, D.C. to attend my first Adventist Association of Family Life Professionals meeting, because I had been elected vice president of public relations.

> Dearest Jill,
> Today is a special day for you. I've finally begun to help you, and you've passed me in accomplishment in an area that's really noticeable, and I just wanted you to know how proud I am of you.
> Though some will never understand, I can readily see why you were selected, and I am glad that others see your special qualities also.
> I also appreciate your loving friendship as a wife and your continual focus on a relationship with the Lord.
> We're proud of you,
> Love, Allan

(Allan) Another treasure from Jill's alabaster box of love is her willingness to be more open—to share more of herself with me and to be my best friend. One would think that after writing, speaking, and presenting seminars together, we would soon know so much about each other that we'd run out of new discoveries. But since we're both changing every day, becoming more and more what God wants us to be, I don't think that will ever happen. Jill and I are looking forward to growing old together and enjoying each day making new discoveries about each other.

(Jill) But it was Allan's unconditional love of me that allowed me to risk being more open.

The first time I sensed a real love from Allan after over ten years of marriage was when I went to the doctor and was told that I needed to change my lifestyle because I was living under too much stress and had developed fibrocystic disease as well as PMS.

I looked at the doctor and said, "What am I supposed to do, leave my husband?" I felt as if I was at my rope's end. I knew much of my stress was caused by the rocky road I was traveling with Allan.

I fell apart. I had always been a strong person. But it was a mask—or more accurately, a full costume—that I was wearing, that said to Allan, "I'll make it regardless of how bad you treat me." When I was affected physically, I realized I could no longer keep doing all the things I was doing to get a little love, and I was crushed. My balloon had burst. If I couldn't do things, I would lose everything I was trying so desperately to hold together.

When I dropped the mask and told Allan, showing my vulnerability, it brought out the softer side of Allan, which I hadn't seen since our courtship days. The months prior to this, he had been lecturing me about losing weight, watching my diet, and exercising. And I just knew he was going to say, "I told you so."

But instead he sat down, put his arm around me, and said, "I love you, even if you have gained a few extra pounds and aren't the happy, carefree person you once were."

Tears filled my eyes. I had waited ten years for this! I

told him I could no longer be superwoman. I had been trying to work my way into doing enough to be worthy of his love. But whatever I did was never enough, because he would never compliment me. So I was driven to do more. Now, because of my health, I had no choice but to slow down. Allan's unconditional love at last was freeing me from the prison of performance. I didn't need the world to rave about my accomplishments. I just needed the man I married to love me.

That's why it was so meaningful to me when he sat there with his arm around me, saying he loved me even though I weighed more and didn't have as much energy as I once had. Allan had broken his alabaster box for me.

I felt I was being courted again as Allan began to bring me red roses every Friday afternoon! But as much as I appreciated the roses, it wasn't the roses that broke the alabaster box for me—it was his giving without expecting anything in return. Just loving me for me—which I had not felt for years. It was the time he took to just sit and listen without trying to fix me by telling me what to do.

Eight years later, I went for my yearly checkup, and another lump had appeared. This time it really looked questionable. Once again I felt overwhelmed. Scared. Questions raced through my head: "Was I going to die? Would my boys be motherless? And would my husband love me less if I had to have a mastectomy?"

It was on the day of our twenty-first wedding anniversary that I received the news about the mass in my left breast. There was a hushed reserve as we ate our special dinner together at the restaurant and later, as we sat in our hotel room, we talked about what the future might hold.

The next day, without our anniversary celebration to think about, the depressing "What if?" feelings crept in. I prayed constantly and forced myself to sing and be happy. But the following day in church, thoughts of possible death and despair hit me, and I broke down. The statistics kept ringing in my ears: After lung cancer, breast cancer is the leading cancer killer of U.S. women: 146,000 a year!

On Sunday, we both went to see the surgeon and were encouraged. He felt that it was possibly another fibrocystic nodule and wanted to see me in two months. He put me on a strict diet and prescribed increased exercise. According to research findings, an extra fifteen pounds increases the risk of breast cancer by 37 percent, and with an extra twenty pounds, the risk increases to 52 percent. That means that a ten-pound difference may be significant when it comes to lowering your cancer risk. And according to Dr. Noreen Azid of the Lee Moffit Cancer Center in Tampa, Florida, of all the decades you should lose that extra weight, it's the third. (That's where I was!)

The weeks passed, and I lost twelve pounds. Allan went with me to see the doctor. An ultrasound and mammogram were done, and the doctor reported, "There is no mass." After comparing the reports and showing us the mammogram, we sighed in relief and sent a prayer heavenward in thanksgiving.

From that experience, we learned how precious our health is and how its threatened loss can suddenly and markedly rearrange our priorities. I now resolve to appreciate each day the Lord gives us and "to be glad and rejoice in it." Knowing that Allan loves me regardless takes away my fear for the future. Our love is secure in sickness and in health.

A strange thing happened to me when Allan began to break his alabaster box of unconditional love for me. At first I was afraid that if I would open up and share what was really on my heart, I might be rejected and wounded once again. But as I risked a little and found it safe, I began to risk more. Then slowly, I began to realize that the things Allan wanted me to do for him, such as keeping the house clean and being on time, were really quite simple. When I didn't *have* to prepare a nice meal to be loved, I found I *wanted* to prepare a lovely meal just because I was loved.

He had previously requested that I remember to keep carrots in the refrigerator, because he wanted four each day for lunch. I was supposed to wash them and put them into a plastic bag for him so they would be ready for his lunch. Such a simple thing, but somehow I never got around to doing it. Once I began to feel loved, however, it was no problem.

Another indication of Allan's willingness to break his alabaster box was when he quit making fun of me and criticizing me in public. All of a sudden he was saying nice things. It was unbelievable. I would look a him and say, "Are you saying that about me?" because it had been so long since he had done that.

An example of this happened when we climbed Mt. Manadnock in New Hampshire in August of 1992. A beautiful, clear blue sky stretched above us, with the wind blowing gently. As we neared the tree line, I looked down momentarily and was surprised at how steep the climb was. Allan, seeing the steepness and knowing the boys had gone ahead, kindly asked, "Shall I go ahead and check on the boys?" I was sure I would be OK, but soon after he left me, I began feeling ill.

When I didn't appear at the top with the other climbers, Allan quickly came back down to check on me. "Allan," I cried, "I can't go up this mountain—I feel as if I'm going to die." I expected his old military style response, "Yes, you can. Just get up and go!" Instead, he encouraged me and said, "I'll help you, Jill." When, with tears in my eyes, I asked if he could get a helicopter to get me off this mountain, he knew I was seriously ill.

He reminded me of the previous evening's program, when I had spoken about turning the terrible into the terrific, and we started laughing about all the good advice I had given. Now I was in a terrible situation and needed some of my own medicine.

He gently took me by my hand, and I followed him down the mountain, keeping my eyes on his back rather than looking down the steep terrain, which was so frightening to me. He gave me just the kind of love and support I needed in my weak moment. As soon as I reached a lower altitude, things began to look terrific once again, especially since Allan allowed me to be me and showed that he loved me even if I couldn't climb to the top.

(Allan) I appreciate Jill more and more each day. Although I used to be jealous of Jill's time spent with the boys, now that they are teenagers, I realize that this investment has paid off, because they are not only our sons but also our good friends. Jill's obvious love and care soft-ened my comments at times and balanced our family. We enjoy communicating and openly sharing about our lives—our hopes, dreams, aspirations, and feelings. I have Jill to thank for that. If I had continued to be the dictator of the home, I doubt I would be enjoying a relationship with my boys now. They would probably have wanted very little to do with me.

Jill's loving and loveable spirit is the best advertisement I know for Christianity. Her genuine care for others, shar-ing herself and her relationship with the Lord, inspires me daily to become more like Him. I'm not a people person to the extent Jill is—I'm more hesitant to approach strang-ers and share the Lord. But I'm learning, thanks to Jill.

Jill's zest for fun and excitement in life has motivated us to do many things that I probably would never have done alone. For example, speaking at a camp meeting in Guadeloupe and going to the Jacques Cousteau Under-water Park there on the island or visiting Butchart Gar-dens after a seminar in Sidney, Vancouver Island. My folks took us only to Washington, D.C., and I'm kind of a home-body.

And now Jill will even go flying with me on occasion, because she loves me—even though I know she's scared! That's commitment!

How thankful I am I woke up before it was too late and recognized that I was putting out the light of Jill's smile because I was so domineering. For years, she was just barely holding on by her fingernails. I'm just so glad she didn't give up on me and that God gave me a second chance.

I've learned that when a relationship isn't going anywhere but down, something's got to change—and the very best place to start is with yourself.

When I began to change my attitude and focus on Jill's needs, giving her the freedom to be herself and feel good about herself, that freedom allowed her to be open to change.

She knew she was loved, and I began to see her smile again and the twinkle in her eyes. I began to hear the joy in her laugh, and she began to have fun and enjoy a good time without wondering if she were going to be put down for being that way. It was just like a flower opening up for the first time.

What I had done was to shut Jill's emotions down. Now, as I have risked it all to love her, she is opening up to me as I never dreamed possible, and I've got that smile back that I first fell in love with—and with it more than I could have ever imagined.

"What ifs" and "If onlys" can imprison you in the past or the future and destroy your chances of experiencing the possibilities of the present! Looking back over Jill's and my life together as married lovers, it would be easy for us to get bogged down with the "What ifs" and "If onlys" and mourn opportunities for love that were spurned and are now forever gone. The same is true if we were to leap forward and worry about the future: "Will we be loved tomorrow when our hair turns gray, our arthritis flares, and our memories lapse?"

As we stand in this chasm in time, the present between two eternities, the past and the future, we only have this moment to enjoy the richness of life. *The precious present!* Jill and I want to make the most of it. Love is a decision we want to make today. We don't want to be conservative, giving each other a little here and a little there, drop by drop. Our desire is to break our alabaster boxes and extravagantly pour out our love on each other.

A house with love in it,
where love is expressed in words and looks and deeds,
is a place where angels love to manifest their presence,
and hallow the scene by rays of light from glory
(E. G. White, *Testimonies for the Church*, 2:417).

Epilogue

Two thousand years ago, when the woman crashed the party, she broke her alabaster box and spilled out its precious contents on the One who had not just saved her life but had given her life *abundantly* by forgiving her rocky road of sin.

Once spilled, her gift could never be retrieved. Her act has perfumed the pages of history, becoming a memorial to those who would aspire to love extravagantly.

We are two of those individuals whose lives have been touched by her act—and like the woman, we want to bring our all to Jesus.

Our alabaster box is this book, the pages of which contain the story of what God's extravagant love has done to transform our lives and to give us life abundantly.

Epilogue

It was not an easy decision to tell it all. We're not proud of the rocky road we have traveled, and we realize that in breaking our box, we've become vulnerable to those who might not understand—just as the woman who crashed the party was misunderstood two thousand years ago.

It is our prayer, however, that our testimony has inspired you to live the life of extravagant love, that the world may be a sweeter place because you have lived—and loved.

Acknowledgments

A special thank you to our parents, Madeline Warren, Frank Evans, and Art and Janice Kennedy for your role and influence in our lives—and to the family members who encouraged us through the years: John and Linda Warren, Judy and Gary Dowker, Jim and Varenda Kennedy, Ann and Ken Shaw, and Jane and Bill Leyva. Because of your love and care, we have love to share.

Thanks to our special friend, Kay Kuzma, for encouraging us to use our talents to help others, inspiring us to share our story, and giving of her valuable time in expertly crafting word pictures to help us not just tell but show our story of extravagant love.

Without our Marriage Encounter (ME) friends, this story could have been never written. We especially want to thank Al and Betty Brendel for bringing ME to the SDA community and for writing such kind words about us in this book. Working with you has been a joy!

To Pastor Dan Stevens for what may have been the shortest and most effective sermon of his ministry, when he said, "Allan, you have a precious flower in Jill. Just make sure you don't crush her." Thank you, Dan, for caring enough to speak up!

Others, too, have been there at significant points in our lives—friends without whom our life journey might have taken a different fork in the road: Mark and Eulita Heisey, Tony and Linda Mavrokas, Duane O'Fill, Faye Clever, Susan Miller, Jane Wright, Frances Earle, Yolanda Oscai, and Dottie Knapp.

From Al and Betty Brendel

Founders of SDA Marriage Encounter

As with all areas of our life—our work, education, family, and even church—marriage has three recurring cycles: romance, disillusionment, and joy. Each of us pass through these stages many times, sometimes more than once in the same day.

In this book, *Longing to be Loved*, Allan and Jill have allowed us to relive these times with them as they discover the great truth that "To Love Is a Decision!"

Each of us brings some brokenness into our relationships and our marriages. Allan and Jill are no exception. Having read their story, you may be reminded of your own marriage and times of romance. Their times of disillusionment and despair may bring a lump to your throat and a tear to your eye. And for some, it may sound all too familiar.

Longing to Be Loved

This is truly a love story, for it embraces commitment, forgiveness, and trust—all made possible because, throughout their painful journey, Allan and Jill held onto God's hand. We have been privileged to present many Marriage Encounter weekends during which Allan and Jill have related parts of their story to the attending couples. Their willingness to make themselves vulnerable has been an act of love to all of us and has brought hope to fellow travelers in their own times of disillusionment.

Because Allan and Jill were not willing that disillusionment be the last word in their marriage but decided instead to work through it rather than run from it, today they experience *joy* in their relationship.

Longing to be Loved is more than just a love story. It is also a challenge for us to look at our own relationships and to learn from our past experiences. It helps us believe that with God "All things are possible" and that He walks the journey with us.

Al and Betty Brendel
Waynesville, Ohio
Marriage Encounter Pastoral Couple

For more information about Marriage Encounter, call 1-800-795-LOVE.

Words From
Kay Kuzma

As I think back to how Jill and I began working together, I still shake my head. It all seems so incredible. I had just finished listening to a group of Polish singers at a program we were both attending and was talking to those who had gathered around. When I saw Jill, I knew we had met before, but I couldn't remember where. So I said, "I can't remember your name."

"Jill Kennedy," she responded. That stimulus brought back a flood of memories: A Marriage Encounter convention. Cohutta Springs, Georgia, July, 1989. Temperatures of 95 degrees and 95 percent humidity, love, and warm southern hospitality.

I remembered how impressed I had been with Jill's genuine concern for others, her bubbly personality, her insight, and the articulate and entertaining way she told about life with her health administrator husband, Allan, and their two boys, Jeremy and Jonathan. Immediately, without thinking, I did something I had never done before. I said, "Jill, I need you to be me!"

My husband, Jan, and I had just moved the Family Matters ministry from Southern California to Cleveland, Tennessee, and I was inundated with requests for speaking appointments. Away almost every weekend, I knew I could not continue this pace. I hadn't really been looking for someone to share this responsibility. That's why I was just as surprised as Jill was with my exclamation. Nothing might have come of it, other than a great story for two sanguines to laugh about later, if Allan hadn't come up at that moment and said, "Jill would be perfect. She's made for that kind of work. I know she could do it!"

Not all husbands are that affirming of their wives' giftedness and skills, especially when it could mean that she would be away from the family when taking out-of-town appointments and when most of the appointments wouldn't bring in much more than the gas money to get there.

But with Allan's encouragement, Jill began listening to my tapes, watching the videos, reading my books to gain a theoretical framework, and then, based on this, spicing her own presentations with the incredible stories of her own life, marriage, and parenting career. Because family is Jill's number one priority, it wasn't long before she began to encourage Allan to join her in this new outreach.

Since 1982, when their marriage began its amazing turnaround at a Marriage Encounter (ME) weekend, they have been actively involved with ME. Not only have they been a presenting team couple but they have willingly accepted the joy of other administrative offices to keep this life-changing ministry alive and growing.

In addition to Marriage Encounter, they have taken many training programs, including Love Takes Time, Developing Capable People, Life Skills, and the certification program for Family Life Education offered through Andrews University. Their combined ministry is indeed powerful.

The more I learned about Jill and Allan's personal story of love lost and found, the more I became convinced that it must be written. I'm sure you identified with the joy and pain they experienced in their struggle to hold together the relationship they were deeply committed to but for far too many years didn't know how to nurture. Surely you laughed as you read about life *way out* in the country of Tennessee and cried as they silently suffered from the sting of rejection and criticism. But in the end, you must have rejoiced over the goodness and power of God to restore the broken and build up the torn down—to bring beauty from ashes.

Most of all, this has been a story of hope for those who are traveling the rocky road of marriage. With the Lord and commitment to each other, you can find fulfillment and experience the extravagant love for which you yearn.

Kay Kuzma, Ed.D.
President of Family Matters
Cleveland, Tennessee

You can contact the Kennedys or Kay Kuzma
about speaking engagements or seminars at:

Family Matters
PO Box 7000
Cleveland, TN 37320
(423) 339-1144

First step on a rocky road
September 2, 1973

Jeremy's first tractor ride.

Eight-month-old Jeremy's Friday
evening bath time in the old trailer.

Allan and Jill Kennedy today.